# Bristol
# LODEKKA

## Martin S. Curtis

Ian Allan
PUBLISHING

# Contents

*Front cover:* Southern Vectis 545 (MDL 955), an LD6G Lodekka built in 1956 with extra luggage capacity for service on the Isle of Wight. When, in the mid-1960s, Bristol offered rear wheel trims, Southern Vectis had these fitted retrospectively to its entire Lodekka fleet. *Ken Jubb*

*Back cover (upper):* Nationalisation of the electricity-supply industry brought into the state sector such companies as Midland General. Its distinctive blue-and-cream livery was well suited to the Lodekka's ECW bodywork, as demonstrated in Nottingham by FSF6G 610 (450 SNU), with later FLF6B 627 (1388 R) behind. *Ken Jubb*

*Back cover (lower):* Brighton, Hove & District 25 (SPM 25), an FS6B, swings past Brighton Aquarium with a full load. It exhibits several features unique to Lodekkas with this company, including a split-level platform, LT-style trafficators, a nearside route-number display and louvres over the sliding windows. *Ken Jubb*

*Previous page:* Scottish operators were often characterised by their use of six-sided route-number/ destination displays, as exemplified by Central SMT BE236 (CGM 736C), a 1965 FLF6G with seating for 68 passengers and an extra luggage rack behind the staircase. *Ken Jubb*

First published 2009

ISBN 978 0 7110 3312 2

Published by Ian Allan Publishing

an imprint of Ian Allan Publishing Ltd, Hersham, Surrey, KT12 4RG

Printed in England by Ian Allan Printing Ltd, Hersham, Surrey, KT12 4RG

Code: 0903/B1

Visit the Ian Allan Publishing website at www.ianallanpublishing.com

# Introduction

THE term 'low-decker' was introduced to me from a very early age by my father. Although having nothing more than the most cursory interest in transport and related matters, my father, Don Curtis, who was an electrical engineer, was familiar with this title (correctly written 'Lodekka'), as he had followed a period of employment with the Great Western Railway by taking a job at what was known colloquially as 'The Construct'.

In the Brislington suburb of Bristol, where I grew up, 'The Construct' was the accepted abbreviation for what had once been the Motor Constructional Works (MCW) of the Bristol Tramways & Carriage Company Ltd but which in 1955 had become Bristol Commercial Vehicles Ltd. My father spent the period from 1947 to 1950 at the MCW, mainly involved with buildings, plant and machinery, but periodically he would tell me that he worked on the electrical wiring of just one bus chassis — the first-ever Lodekka.

With nationalisation of the works and the fear of reduced orders my father — and many of his colleagues — decided to seek employment elsewhere, and he thus moved to the chocolate factory of J. S. Fry & Sons, of Somerdale, Keynsham (over the county boundary in Somerset), where in later years he served as Electrical Engineer for the site. We continued to live in Brislington, however, and it so happened that the bus route which passed our house was the 36, which during much of my child-hood was maintained by Bristol Lodekkas, including none other than LHY 949 — the very first prototype worked on by my dad. This bus was withdrawn and, regrettably, scrapped in 1963 but had in the meantime been followed by hundreds of production models, including longer, and forward-entrance versions of the Lodekka design. The last of these had evolved into what, to me, were incredibly attractive vehicles, due to constant subtle improvements in detailing from the Bristol and ECW designers.

Apart from its low overall height, increasingly taken for granted was the Lodekka's low, step-less entrance, which permitted fast boarding and alighting for everyone but, for the elderly in particular, allowed this process to remain a relatively easy affair. When encountering other designs elsewhere, most notably forward-entrance Routemaster RMF1254 at London (Heathrow) Airport in 1965, I was horrified to see that several steps had to be climbed in order to reach the lower saloon. It was then that I realised just how clever the Bristol designers had been.

Like all Brislington residents of the period, I was familiar with the sight of Lodekkas in chassis form running around on test or heading, as I discovered, for Lowestoft, where bodywork was fitted. There were also occasional family

With driver protected against the elements, an FLF Lodekka chassis climbs Kensington Hill at speed during December 1966 as it leaves Brislington at the start of its 265-mile journey to Eastern Coach Works at Lowestoft. Note the Cave-Browne-Cave radiator mounted high behind the driver. *Mike Walker*

Uphill Wharf, on the edge of Weston-super-Mare, is the delightful setting for two Bristol Lodekkas from the local Bristol Omnibus Co fleet, on layover in the early 1960s. On the left is L8434 (YHT 950), a 1957 LD6B, while alongside is 8578 (868 NHT), a 1961 FS6G with convertible-open-top bodywork. *A. Dewfall*

excursions from Bristol, to locations where it was still possible to see the familiar shape of Lodekka buses, albeit displaying unfamiliar fleetnames — and some were even painted red! Gradually it became clear that Bristol also built buses for companies both near and far from home.

I therefore grew up with Lodekkas. They were built on my doorstep and became an increasingly important part of my life. They carried me and my family into town (central Bristol) and in my teenage years provided my daily transport to and from school. After joining the Bristol Omnibus Co as a traffic clerk I found myself working alongside Lodekkas, eventually conducting and driving them until, later still, following a move to the Western National Omnibus Co, I was managing examples of the type.

Today, with friends and colleagues from the bus preservation movement, I am involved in owning, restoring and running examples at rallies or special events — sometimes with my son Tom at the wheel.

It is some 60 years since the first chassis was wired by a member of the Curtis family, but for me the Bristol Lodekka remains one of the cleverest bus designs ever conceived.

*Martin S. Curtis* FCILT, M Inst TA
Saltford, Bristol
May 2008

## Acknowledgements

IT WOULD BE impossible to produce a book of this kind without the help and support of others. However, in the preparation of this volume the generosity of so many friends and colleagues has been overwhelming.

Fellow Bristol enthusiasts Geoff Bruce, Allen Janes, Allan Macfarlane, Phil Sposito, Mike Walker and Dave Withers have provided enormous help by checking drafts or sourcing photographs for inclusion. Each picture has been individually credited, but further information or assistance was provided by Dave Allen, John Banks, David Bruce, Chris Brown, Stephen Cho, Allan Condie, Mike Davis, Phil Davies, Maurice Doggett, Mike Eyre, Allan Field, Paul Lacey, Mike Mogridge, Alan Neale, Don Ottrey, Jasper Petty, Rob Sly, Stuart Russell, Ian Semple, Chris Stewart, Alan Townsin and Robin Wilding, many of whom provided leads which resulted in a source of information or the discovery of a long-lost photograph. Kevin McCormack provided photographs by John May, and Tony Wilson, of Travel Lens Photographic, produced prints by Geoff Lumb, while information concerning Midland General-group vehicles came from David Bean, Paul Chambers, Bob Gell and Arthur Webb. Eastern Coach Works photographs from the pre-1960 era are now owned by Simon Butler, while later subjects have in some cases been obtained from Brian Ollington Photographers.

Further detailed information or access to records was provided by Bristol Record Office, Bristol Reference Library, The Omnibus Society and the PSV Circle.

# 1 Before the Lodekka

THE double-decker bus is a peculiarly British phenomenon. True, since the beginning of the 21st century such vehicles have become slightly less dominant than they once were, and certainly double-deckers can be found abroad, but it is Great Britain with which they have always been most associated, never more so than in the period immediately following World War 2.

The 'omnibus', offering travel 'for all', is generally acknowledged as having first appeared in 1829 with the commencement of George Shillibeer's London service between Paddington and the Bank of England. This, of course, was horse-drawn, and similar 'buses' began to appear all over London and elsewhere. By the 1840s male passengers would sometimes travel on the roof of horse-buses, but with the advent of the Great Exhibition in 1851 the public demand for travel was such that additional seating was increasingly provided 'on top', and the double-decker bus was born.

The design of open-top, double-deck horse buses progressed from that point, with more passengers accommodated if seating were arranged facing forward rather than longitudinally.

Mechanically propelled vehicles arrived from the turn of the century, powered initially by petrol, electricity or steam, but by 1910 petrol-engined vehicles had proved to be the most popular, and horse-buses were being rapidly replaced by motor buses. Initially these machines had their engines located where the horses had been — in front! However, it was soon realised that by positioning the engine alongside the driver, more passenger space could be created, and when pneumatic tyres were widely adopted from the mid-1920s, passenger comfort also increased.

An early example of a double-decker motor bus. Introduced by Bristol Tramways in 1906, this FIAT is seen at Brislington Square, about to embark on its journey to Keynsham and Saltford. Such vehicles were not a success mechanically, but, convinced of the merits of motor traction, the company began building its own design of motor buses two years later.
*Bristol Evening Post*

The 'invention' of the double-decker bus was followed almost immediately by attempts to lower its overall height, especially once it was fitted with an upper-deck roof. However, in London in particular, double-deckers generally remained open-top for a little longer, the Metropolitan Police requiring much convincing that adding a roof to such a vehicle was a safe step to take. Improvements in chassis-frame design, to lower the saloon floor level and thereby reduce overall

height, assisted greatly in overcoming these concerns. In the provinces, acceptance of covered upper decks had generally been rather more forthcoming, although the Cheltenham District Traction Co was prevented by the local town council from taking delivery of covered-top double-deckers until as late as 1934, which was only two years before the newly formed Brighton, Hove & District Omnibus Co led the world with the reintroduction of open-top double-deckers on seafront routes to cater specifically for holidaymakers and tourists.

The manufacture of buses by the Bristol company had begun in 1908. Production intensified from 1912 following the establishment of the Motor Constructional Works at Brislington, and increasingly buses were built not only for the Bristol Tramways & Carriage Co but for other operators also.

The first Bristol double-deckers were built in 1923 on 4-ton chassis for Hull Corporation. Although also producing its own bodywork, when the Bristol Tramways company was absorbed into the Tilling group from the early 1930s, a very special relationship was to develop with another

Tilling company, Eastern Coach Works of Lowestoft, and by the 1940s collaboration between the two concerns had reached a point where it was difficult to determine whether Bristol/ECW constituted two manufacturers or just one.

Throughout the first half of the 20th century Britain retained an extensive railway network, and this resulted in vast numbers of low bridges to carry the railways across the increasingly busy roads. As the desire to operate double-decker buses increased to cater for growing passenger numbers, such bridges, along with other overhead obstructions, often presented a serious obstacle for bus operators. In some areas numerous low bridges would be encountered in quick succession, but, in any case, it required only one low bridge on an important route to prevent the use of double-decker buses.

A partial solution to the problem came in the late 1920s. By this time most closed-top double-deckers were being built to an overall height of around 15ft, with, on both decks, rows of forward-facing double seats either side of a central gangway. In 1927, however, Leyland introduced its highly successful Titan TD1, which was available with double-deck bodywork built to a design that became known as 'lowbridge'. This retained a central gangway downstairs but on the upper deck featured four-abreast seating, with a sunken gangway running along the offside. The reduction in overall height thus achieved was in excess of 12in, and in a great many cases this was sufficient to enable operators to introduce double-deckers on routes with over-bridges or other overhead obstructions.

The lowbridge design nevertheless had some serious disadvantages which made such buses increasingly unpopular with both passengers and crews. On the upper deck, passengers furthest away from the gangway often found that, in order to vacate their seat, they had to disturb three other passengers. Moreover, upper-deck headroom was very limited: passengers would frequently bang their heads on the ceiling and, when seated, found that the top of the windows was below eye level, severely limiting forward and side visibility, especially on a full bus; conductors, meanwhile, found fare collection difficult, frequently having to reach over other passengers in order to collect cash or issue tickets. In the lower saloon the sunken side gangway significantly reduced headroom for passengers seated beneath it on the offside, leading to more banging of heads!

Despite the disadvantages, the lowbridge double-decker represented a solution to a problem that would otherwise have barred large-capacity buses from many services, and, as passenger

numbers grew, this became increasingly important. Other attempts at lowering overall height had been less successful, one of the most radical being produced by the Gilford Motor Co, of High Wycombe, which at the 1931 Commercial Motor Show at Olympia displayed a front-wheel-drive double-decker. Built to an overall height no greater than that of a lowbridge Leyland Titan, this offered forward-facing seating and a central gangway on both decks, but it was ahead of its time and failed to attract any orders. The lowbridge layout was therefore adopted by all manufacturers as an alternative to the conventional arrangement, and, whilst there were numerous exceptions, conventional 'highbridge' vehicles usually held sway in towns and cities, the lowbridge design becoming more familiar in rural areas.

Despite a desperate need for more vehicles in many areas, the availability of new buses was severely disrupted by World War 2, manufacturers being directed to concentrate on production directly related to the war effort, and several bus-building firms were additionally involved in aircraft assembly. Among these latter was Bristol — not unnaturally, for the Bristol Aeroplane Co and Bristol Tramways concerns had been closely related, being effectively 'cousins' sharing a common ancestry; it was for this reason that each displayed on its products and services the Bristol scroll insignia.

While, in the immediate postwar era of the late 1940s, Britain had still to recover from a period of austerity, many of the country's engineers found themselves making rapid technological advances, having developed new skills and techniques at an incredible rate throughout the years of hostility. Nothing better illustrates this than aircraft design, which in little more than 50 years had developed from the earliest flying machines to reliable jet-powered aircraft. In the motor industry also, technical awareness had increased hugely, and bus builders were among those to benefit most, there being some surprising similarities between aircraft construction and bus manufacture, notably in the use of new lightweight materials, jig-building to ensure accuracy and speed of assembly, and an improved knowledge of stress factors and material strength.

The need urgently to replace worn-out fleets meant that bus building was undertaken with vigour after the war, and the new manufacturing methods were employed as materials became available, designs being revised as a consequence. Innovative ideas seemed to be bursting off the draughtsmen's drawing boards, nowhere more so than at Bristol Tramways and Eastern Coach Works. Nevertheless, Bristol's postwar double-decker remained the diesel-engined K type, which, although updated, had actually been introduced before the war, in 1937. This was becoming the standard model for both Tilling group customers and others, including several prominent municipalities. It was built initially to a length of 26ft and width of 7ft 6in, the maximum then generally permitted for a two-axle double-decker (although

Postwar Britain saw vast numbers of passengers using overstretched services, while vehicles were run-down and in need of overhaul or replacement. In order to record patterns of passenger movements Bristol Tramways extensively photographed its busiest locations. This view, recorded at mid-day on Saturday 29 December 1945, showing K type C3259 (GAE 457) with the company's own bodywork, illustrates the constant strain under which all services found themselves.
*Bristol Tramways*

*Above:* Illustrating the difference between 'highbridge' and 'lowbridge' bodywork, these two Bristol/ECW KSWs (C8320 and L8089) from the Bristol Omnibus Vehicle Collection show how the revised internal arrangements resulted in significant variations in overall height. *M. S. Curtis*

*Right:* The interior upper deck of a conventional highbridge bus, showing the central aisle with double seats on either side. This is a Bristol/ECW KSW built in 1950. *ECW*

*Left:* Employed in order to reduce overall height by around 12 inches, the lowbridge layout involved four-abreast seating on the top deck, with limited headroom, and a side gangway sunken into the saloon below.
*ECW*

*Left:* Both highbridge and lowbridge styles of bodywork had central gangways on the lower deck and a step down onto the rear platform. As apparent from this view, lowbridge buses unfortunately had the disadvantage of reduced headroom along the offside, owing to the sunken gangway above. This is an Eastern Coach Works-bodied Bristol K.
*ECW*

special dispensation was granted for a small batch of 8ft-wide KW models to operate in Cardiff from 1948). However, with a relaxation from 1950 of maximum vehicle dimensions there appeared a longer, 27ft KS version, the increase in length being used partly to accommodate more comfortably six- (rather than five-) cylinder diesel engines from manufacturers such as Gardner. Also produced was a long, wide variant, the KSW, which took advantage of the increased maximum width for buses of 8ft. Bodywork nevertheless continued to follow the (by now) established highbridge or lowbridge patterns, depending upon the routes selected for their operation. It remained the case, therefore, that as passenger numbers continued to grow, the inconvenience of the awkward lowbridge layout was still a source of considerable frustration.

# 2 Prototypes and trials

THE Commercial Vehicle Exhibition held at Earl's Court, London, in October 1948 featured an impressive display by Bristol Tramways' Motor Constructional Works, which had six vehicles on its stand. Prominent were the company's K (double-deck) and L (single-deck) models, the former being represented by an Eastern Coach Works-bodied example in the livery of the Lincolnshire Road Car Co. Of the three L types, one was finished to the specification of United Automobile Services, while reflecting Bristol's involvement in the substantial export drive then being encouraged by the Government was a bare chassis which was part of a large order for India; alongside this was a completed wide, long LWL destined for South Africa, another market in which Bristol was achieving considerable success. These chassis were powered by either Gardner or Bristol's own diesel engines, which resulted in a number and letter code following the chassis type to denote the number of cylinders and engine manufacturer. Thus the full type designation of the double-decker, with six-cylinder Bristol engine, was K6B.

The K and L models on the stand were accompanied by two examples of a new Bristol model, the M type, both of which appeared in chassis form. A double-deck MD6G was Gardner-powered, while a single-deck Bristol-engined MSW6B was built to a wide specification, again with export markets in mind. Both featured wide radiators of a new design, with chrome-plated surround, and prominent front bumper bars. However, neither chassis was to receive bodywork, nor did the M type ever enter production. Moreover, as will be explained, the company would not be permitted to exhibit at future commercial motor shows for almost two decades.

Postwar Britain saw the election of a Labour government with a mandate to nationalise much of the country's transport services, including the railways, inland waterways, road haulage and, of course, bus and coach services. This resulted in the establishment, following the Transport Act 1947,

of the British Transport Commission. The view was taken by the Tilling group — which included 20 bus-operating companies together with some goods and motor-hire interests (with a combined fleet total of around 8,000 vehicles), in addition to the manufacturing facilities of Bristol and ECW — that it would be preferable to sell its road transport interests to the state voluntarily, rather than wait to find itself compelled to dispose of its assets to the BTC. During September 1948, only one month before the 1948 Show, the decision of the Thomas Tilling organisation was announced, and whilst this resulted in considerable uncertainty, it was not immediately apparent that the effects on Bristol and ECW manufacturing were to be particularly significant.

Among the provisions of the 1947 Act was a clause, sought by the Opposition, which resulted in restrictions on sales of Bristol and ECW products to customers outside the state-owned sector, save for orders already on the books at the time of nationalisation. This immediately halted sales of Bristol and ECW products to numerous bus companies and municipalities, including a number of loyal customers, and instantly scuppered Bristol's promising export trade, which had been considered an important contribution to the nation's economy. Some ill feeling was also generated among other vehicle manufacturers (although quite why is less clear), and Bristol was placed under some pressure to resign from the Society of Motor Manufacturers & Traders (SMMT), an organisation of which the company had been a member for some 40 years. However, the restrictions failed to dampen Bristol's or ECW's enthusiasm or commitment for innovation and new ideas, and the next few years would witness the emergence from Bristol and Lowestoft of some of the most revolutionary and influential designs ever seen in the bus industry.

Thoughts of producing a greatly improved low-height double-decker had been progressing even before the 1948 Motor Show, the unveiling of the M-type design or the impact of nationalisation,

with its sales restrictions, had been fully absorbed. Already the company had applied for patents (to be followed by others) covering the design of a bus with closely integrated chassis and body sides, a low frame and driving axle, and split transmission lines of alternative designs, all of which would combine to form the basis of a new low-height vehicle. These patents were applied for jointly and variously in the names of the Bristol Tramways Co, the works manager and senior designers.

During the summer of 1949 careful assembly of the first prototype was undertaken in the company's experimental shop at its Bath Road works. This chassis was then sent to Lowestoft for bodying, the completed vehicle being recorded by ECW's official photographer on 2 September. Finished in a version of Bristol Tramways' own Tilling green and cream livery, this bus was registered LHY 949 and, in a break with tradition for a Bristol chassis, was given a model name — Lodekka — derived, of course, from the term 'low decker'.

Full details of the innovative new model immediately appeared in print, including a story by Mr A. J. Romer, General Manager of the Bristol Motor Constructional Works and one of the names appearing on a number of the patent applications, in the works' own magazine, *The Gazette*, for October 1949. The trade press also published major stories about the new Bristol design, *Commercial Motor*, in its 7 October issue, heralding it as 'The end of the low-roof double-decker', while *Bus & Coach*, in its January 1950 number, emphasised that it was the *nationalised* Bristol Tramways company whose design overcame the chief objections to the lowbridge type. A new enthusiasts' publication with the title *Buses Illustrated* also gave an account of the design, in what was only its second issue, dated Jan-Feb 1950. Describing the design as 'One of the most important developments of recent months', it included a diagram demonstrating that a normal highbridge bus of the period was just under 14ft 4in tall, whereas the Lodekka matched the height of a lowbridge vehicle, achieving slightly less than 13ft 4in. Even the *Bristol Evening Post* announced the appearance of the design to the Bristol public at large, with a story entitled 'New bus for low bridge routes' on 30 September 1949, which, significantly, was the day the bus was viewed in Central London, displaying Bristol-area destinations! It had been driven up from Bristol and was seen turning out from London Transport's Victoria garage, to be inspected by members of the British Transport Commission.

**Bristol's stand at the 1948 Commercial Motor Show. Nearest the camera are the company's two M-type chassis, which were destined never to receive bodywork. They display new, wide radiators, which were later to appear on the Lodekka prototypes.**
*Bristol Tramways*

The first prototype Lodekka chassis, PT149, which was later redesignated LDX.001, photographed during testing in 1949. Clearly visible are the down-swept cross-members and rear axle, to accommodate the sunken gangway, while the propeller shaft runs along the offside from the clutch housing until dividing mid-way along the chassis. *Bristol Tramways*

The Lodekka designers had cleverly combined the benefits of a lowbridge bus with the characteristics of a highbridge vehicle to produce a bus of low overall height which nevertheless retained a central gangway on both decks. Furthermore, the lower-deck gangway was much lower than on previous bus designs, which feature eliminated the step between the rear platform and the lower saloon. Not only was the Lodekka's design more convenient and comfortable for passengers; it was also more accessible for the elderly and infirm and increased the rate of passenger flow within the vehicle by removing several obstacles which hitherto had hindered internal passenger movement, at a stroke rendering obsolete the internal layout of previous double-deck designs. This was achieved by lowering the lower-saloon floor, with centrally down-swept cross members and a new design of dropped-centre rear axle, the drive to

which was divided mid-way along the chassis allowing the gangway to be placed at an extremely low level and slightly sunken below the remainder of the floor. This involved offsetting the main propeller shaft to the offside, which split mid-way along the chassis frame where it met a cross-driving unit containing the differential gears. From here two drivelines continued independently to the rear axle. That on the offside remained on a relatively straight course, while the other was taken across the chassis and turned through 90° using bevel gears, to run along the nearside.

The rear axle had separate worm and worm-wheel reduction gears for the final drive to each set of rear wheels, while the axle's centre beam was swept down to pass under the low gangway. Some thought had been given to the possibility of adopting front-wheel drive, but this was considered undesirable and instead led eventually to the above arrangement.

The dropped-centre rear axle was cast from aluminium alloys (as were other chassis components) in order to keep weight as low as possible, but its shape represented a radical departure. The Experimental Department was therefore required to test the Design Office's creation to destruction, to ensure that the pioneering design would withstand the pressures and strains it would have to endure in everyday service. Undertaking this task involved close co-operation with the Bristol Aeroplane Company, which lent strain-measuring instruments and supplied personnel to attend the testing. The behaviour of the casting was closely observed and recorded in a similar manner to the testing of aircraft components, while the axle was subjected to more than five times its expected service load.

The floor itself was applied directly to the chassis frame, requiring close collaboration with the bodybuilder. The relationship between Bristol and ECW ensured that the two were already ideally placed in this respect, allowing the light-alloy body frame to combine with the chassis to create a semi-integral unit.

The Lodekka's lower floor resulted in increased protrusion into the lower saloon of the rear wheel-arches, accommodated initially by incorporating large luggage racks, while similar intrusion from the gearbox, immediately aft of the engine, was disguised by a rearward-facing seat for five passengers. The driving position was also significantly lower than on earlier bus designs and incorporated a more raked-back steering wheel, offering what was sometimes described as a car-like driving position.

The level of the lower deck having been reduced, it was a relatively simple matter to

201 HT

construct an upper saloon with central gangway without exceeding the overall height constraints. The new Lodekka accommodated 58 passengers — three more than usual for a lowbridge bus — and was powered by a Bristol AVW 8.25-litre engine. The complete vehicle weighed 7 tons 9½cwt.

From the point of view of the general public, the Lodekka bus was clearly something different, as lower-deck passengers found themselves much lower in relation to pedestrians or queuing passengers waiting to board. Once on the platform, passengers regularly stamped hard on the floor (to the amusement of many) as they entered the lower saloon, so used were they to stepping up at this point! And a new bus design of this significance mattered greatly to most of the population, as this was the era of widespread bus use by almost everyone in society, bus patronage growing further during the 1950s.

*Above:* The bodywork of LDX.001 under construction at Eastern Coach Works, Lowestoft. Close co-operation between Bristol and ECW was essential, as the rigidity of the finished vehicle was dependent on the body structure acting as an extension of the chassis. *Phil Sposito collection*

*Left:* An interior view of the first Lodekka's lower deck, clearly showing how the sunken gangway led directly onto the platform without a downward step, as was the case on other types of double-decker. *ECW*

*Left:* The upper deck of the first Lodekka, illustrating the inclusion of a central gangway despite the low overall height of the vehicle. Seat coverings were of the standard Tilling pattern for the period. *ECW*

**THE GAZETTE**

VOL

NUMBER

OCTOBER 1949

PRICE SIXPENCE

A "Bristol"—Eastern Coach Works Achievement

*In this issue*

A Date with a Dowser

The New "Lodekka" Bus

Pin-pricks ruined Tramways Soccer

The Armoured Brigade

The Maintenance Gazette

ALL THE NEWS AND PICTURES OF THE MONTH

OFFICIAL ORGAN OF THE BRISTOL TRAMWAYS & CARRIAGE CO. LTD. MOTOR CONSTRUCTIONAL WORKS SPORTS CLUB

*Above:* The first prototype, LHY 949, received fleet number C5000 and had entered service with Bristol Tramways by the end of 1949. Almost a year later, in October 1950, it is here descending Park Street, with the University of Bristol's Wills Tower dominating the scene. *Peter Davey*

*Below:* Another view of C5000 shortly after entering trial service on routes 2/2A. The staff member talking to the driver can look down at the lower-deck passengers, something not possible on earlier types, while upstairs passengers sit high above the window line. *M. Mogridge*

The first Lodekka prototype (chassis number PT.149, though this was soon changed to LDX.001) was allocated to Bristol's own fleet as No C5000 (LHY 949). By the end of March 1950 a second Bristol-engined prototype had been completed (with chassis number LDX.002) to the same overall dimensions, with a body 7ft 6in wide and 26ft long. The wheelbase of the LDXs was 15ft 11in. Both prototypes featured the same design of wide radiator as first seen on the M types, and indeed it is believed that the radiators used were actually transferred from the M-type chassis. The second prototype was finished in the Tilling-red and cream of the West Yorkshire Road Car Co, registered JWT 712 and allocated fleet number 822. This vehicle incorporated a slightly different version of transmission featuring a differential behind the gearbox, from which two full-length propeller shafts ran on either side of the chassis frame to the worm-drive units located on each side

*Above:* The October 1949 edition of *The Gazette*, the Motor Constructional Works' house magazine, with the first Lodekka featured on the cover.

of the rear axle. ECW's bodywork was also slightly revised with much taller windows and the elimination of the small quarter windows towards the rear of the lower deck. The increased window depth resulted in shallower roof domes and the cream relief was applied as two between-decks bands in the style established on K-type vehicles.

The collaboration between Bristol and ECW was probably never closer than during the development of the Lodekka, as was evident in the lower saloon, further modifications being incorporated into the gangway area compared to the first prototype. The gangway itself was significantly wider but more cluttered than before, with the appearance of additional casings to house some of the transmission and chassis components, although the intrusions were reduced over the rear axle.

It was planned that further Lodekka prototypes should follow. The works register for this period shows that two additional, experimental Lodekkas were proposed, with notes for parts to be set aside for up to ten further chassis. However, no more Lodekkas were built until thorough testing of LDX.001 and LDX.002 had been undertaken, and a production design settled upon, even though operators were keen to purchase buses built to Bristol's new low-height layout.

There were several reasons why further Lodekkas did not follow immediately. One was that Bristol was simultaneously developing another new passenger chassis, which was to become the LS single-decker, with underfloor engine. This was followed by the design and construction of eight-wheel heavy-goods chassis for the Road Haulage Executive, which organisation traded as British Road Services. With the loss of bus and coach orders from outside the state-controlled sector, the works' spare capacity was to be used for the construction of lorry chassis to the requirements of the nationalised road-haulage operators. This — and sub-contract work for the Bristol Aeroplane Co, British Railways and London Transport — nevertheless failed to prevent a significant reduction in overall output from the Bristol works during this period, with associated loss of jobs. Finally, there was a chronic shortage of raw materials as industry re-established itself following the war years, and

*Right:* West Yorkshire's Lodekka was displayed at the Festival of Britain during 1951 and is pictured here at the exhibition, where it was inspected by thousands of visitors. At that time buses generally played a much more prominent role in the lives of almost everyone in society than is the case today. *R. H. G. Simpson*

*Right:* The activities of Bristol Tramways were always closely followed by the local press, and the introduction of LHY 949 onto the streets of Bristol was sufficiently important to justify sending out a photographer. This head-on view of the bus on a heavily-laden journey to Stapleton Church offers the opportunity to study some of the detail of the first prototype. *Bristol Evening Post*

*Above:* A comparison with the second prototype, JWT 712, can be made while it is viewed awaiting departure for Leeds. Deeper windows and a shallower roof dome are apparent, while the three-piece destination display contrasts with the Bristol Tramways type. *G. F. Ashwell*

*Left:* Photographs of the Lodekka prototypes on loan to operators are surprisingly scarce. Among the most successful visits was that of LHY 949 to Scottish Omnibuses, which eventually resulted in the purchase of hundreds of production models. This view was recorded in St Andrew Square, Edinburgh. *©Scottish Motor Museum Trust. Licensor www. scran. ac. uk*

this frequently resulted in planned production being cut back, owing to a shortage of essential materials or components.

The benefit of this situation for the Lodekka was that the design was tested extensively before production commenced. The company minutes of 14 February 1951 reported that 30,000 miles had been completed by the West Yorkshire vehicle while the Bristol prototype had reached 40,000 miles, and both prototypes were then undertaking a tour of operating companies. The first LDX, Bristol C5000, was loaned to several other BTC companies, including Eastern National, Hants & Dorset, Thames Valley, Westcliff-on-Sea, Western National, Wilts & Dorset and, in Scotland, W. Alexander & Sons and Scottish Motor Traction; these latter were particularly significant, since the newly nationalised Scottish companies, unlike those of the Tilling group, were not familiar with Bristol products. The second LDX prototype appeared at Brislington during April 1950, immediately after completion, and was then despatched to Brighton, Hove & District before eventually reaching Yorkshire. Later, during 1951, this bus visited other operators, including Crosville, Cumberland, Eastern Counties, Lincolnshire, Mansfield District, Midland General, Notts & Derby, United Automobile and United Counties, the intention being that each BTC operator should have the opportunity to try one of the prototypes.

To boost trade and industry's postwar recovery during the early 1950s, the Festival of Britain was held on London's South Bank, and West Yorkshire's Lodekka was selected for display at this prestigious event from 24 August to 30 September

1951, as were other British-built buses which took turns to appear at other times. Both LDXs then settled down to full working lives with their respective owners, the Bristol example regularly working Bristol city route 36 from Old Market to Brislington, Knowle and, later, Withywood; coincidentally the West Yorkshire example often appeared on another service 36, between Harrogate and Leeds. Despite their non-standard and experimental nature, the West Yorkshire example remained in service until the summer of 1962, while Bristol LC5000 (as it had by now become) continued to give good service until March 1963. Regrettably, both of these revolutionary vehicles were scrapped following withdrawal.

*Above:* An astonishing picture, taken by chance, revealed that LHY 949 operated for Griffin Motors, an associate company of the newly nationalised Red & White concern. It is seen displaying destination linens for 'Cwm via Brynmawr', shortly before Griffin was absorbed by Red & White under state control. *Peter Davey collection*

*Right:* Westcliff-on-Sea Motor Services was among many established Tilling operators to try out the first Lodekka prototype, here seen running to Shoeburyness; as usual a paper sticker in the front nearside window indicates its status as a vehicle 'on loan' to the local operator. While in Edinburgh this bus ran under tramway overhead power lines, but in this view it is beneath trolleybus wires. *R. F. Mack*

*Below:* The second prototype (JWT 712) was operated on trial with the Midland General group of companies. It appears in this view on Mansfield District's route 101, alongside an AEC Regent III from the local fleet, with highbridge bodywork built by Weymann.
*Photograph: G. H. F. Atkins, courtesy & © John Banks collection*

*Above:* A rare colour photograph of LHY 949, taken at Bristol's Marlborough Street bus station in June 1960. By this time its fleet number had become LC5000.
*M. Mogridge*

*Left:* Sold for scrap! Beyond the remains of a Crossley in the foreground, JWT 712 is dismantled for scrap during 1962; a year later a similar fate befell LHY 949. It is a matter of great regret that neither prototype was saved for posterity.
*The JSC Archive*

# 3 Pre-production models

WHILE testing of the prototype Lodekkas continued, many Tilling operators became increasingly anxious to introduce this revolutionary model, which would see an end to the unpopular and inconvenient lowbridge layout. However, where height restrictions prevailed, they were compelled for the time being to replenish their fleets with more buses of the lowbridge design, for the reasons outlined in the last chapter. Indeed, those that had specifically ordered Lodekkas for 1952 delivery, including Bristol Tramways' own operating department, were asked to accept lowbridge K-series vehicles instead. One consequence was that BTCC introduced a batch of 10 lowbridge KSWs, which were to remain unique in its fleet.

By December 1951 further re-design work for the Lodekka was progressing well in the light of experience with the prototypes, and by March 1952, despite ongoing shortages of materials, orders for the supplies required to commence production of the new chassis were being placed with the aim of instigating Lodekka production during the second half of 1953.

Orders were then invited from operators for the 1953 programme, and those wanting Lodekkas were accepted in anticipation of full production commencing. Over 140 had been requested by the summer of 1952 and the Bristol Tramways & Carriage Co minutes of 26 September record that 'Energetic measures were being taken to obtain the materials to produce six pre-production Lodekka chassis by the end of this year, preparatory to general production commencing mid-1953'.

Naturally these vehicles were to have ECW bodies, and by December 1952 everything was prepared to start assembly with the vehicles to be ready for service in the early spring. One would of

The first of the pre-production Lodekkas naturally went to Bristol Tramways' own fleet, to become L8133 (PHW 958). Shortly after entering service, it is here about to depart from what was then Bristol's major country bus terminus in Prince Street, on the busy service 27 to Wells, Glastonbury and Street. *R. F. Mack*

course be allocated to Bristol's own fleet while the others were destined for operators who had already ordered the type for 1953. Appropriately, this included West Yorkshire so they too could compare the intended production design with their LDX, whilst in any case, arrangements were once more being made to loan the pre-production vehicles to other companies in the group, allowing each the opportunity of studying the improvements to the design.

The first two pre-production chassis were delivered to Lowestoft for bodying during February 1953. Bristol chassis were built in sanctions of typically 100, 200 or 250 chassis, and the pre-production Lodekkas, all powered by Bristol's own AVW engine, were allocated at the beginning of the 100th sanction. The 'LD' designation was to apply in addition to the Lodekka name, Bristol-engined examples thus becoming LD6B types. The remaining pre-production chassis reached Lowestoft during March or April, the batch of six receiving the following identities:

100.001  Bristol Tramways L8133 (PHW 958)
100.002  Crosville ML661 (RFM 406)
100.003  Hants & Dorset 1337 (LRU 67)
100.004  United Counties 950 (JBD 955)
100.005  West Yorkshire DX2 (MWR 618)
100.006  Western National 1863 (OTT 2)

All were therefore finished in Tilling green and cream with the exception of the West Yorkshire vehicle, which was the solitary red example.

Compared with the original prototypes the pre-production Lodekkas offered a range of improvements. Firstly, they were longer and wider than the LDXs, reflecting revisions to the maximum vehicle dimensions allowing double-deckers to be 27ft long and 8ft wide. However, the most important changes concerned the transmission. This had been modified further following the extensive trials with the earlier prototypes and now employed a simplified arrangement with a single propeller shaft running down the offside of the chassis. At its forward end, it was coupled to an output shaft on the gearbox which was offset to the right. A five-speed constant-mesh gearbox was employed, with a four-speed unit available as an alternative. The propeller shaft ran to the rear of the chassis to connect with an entirely new design of dropped-centre rear axle. Spur gears were located on either side of the axle with differential and spiral bevel primary reduction gear also located inside the offside casing. Power was therefore taken to the offside road wheels, with a shaft contained within the axle leading from the differential to the spur gears on the nearside. Instead of taking the drive separately to either side of the rear axle, as in the prototypes, the new arrangement involved a single

*Above:* A rear offside view of Hants & Dorset 1337 (LRU 67), another of the six pre-production Lodekkas, illustrating the considerable revisions to styling compared to the prototypes. The unmistakable ECW look nevertheless remained. *ECW*

*Right:* All of the pre-production Lodekkas had open rear platforms. With a stepless entrance from the platform into the lower saloon, Bristol and ECW were setting standards that other manufacturers could not easily match. *ECW*

driveline, the drive passing from the offside to the nearside rear wheels within the axle itself. These modifications, together with further changes to the chassis frame, allowed further improvements to the gangway arrangement and eliminated the slightly inward-sloping floor in the lower saloon.

Gone too was the wide radiator and bonnet of the earlier LDXs, as Bristol had developed an enclosed bonnet and cowl which concealed the radiator, made of glass-reinforced plastic (or fibre glass), a material adopted widely for the cabs of Bristol lorries from about this time. An outline of a radiator with vertical slots occupied the full depth of the cowl and had a very heavy appearance. As on Bristol's conventional, exposed-radiator models, a cast '*Bristol*' scroll badge appeared at 45° across the offside top corner, while an oval '*Bristol*' scroll badge was retained at the top of the radiator outline, with an ECW badge positioned in the centre of the lower edge. This outline was similar to that introduced the previous year on Bristol lorries.

*Above:* Considerable attention was given to improving the lower-saloon interior, compared to the prototypes. A wider gangway was maintained, with many of the cover plates and other intrusions eliminated. Luggage racks remained next to the rear, side-facing bench seats, while a host of minor detail modifications combined to offer an extremely attractive interior which disguised the level of innovation under the floor! *ECW*

*Left:* United Counties' example, 950 (JBD 955), resting between duties. As with other Lodekkas, the front wings had been shortened, as eventually became standard on production versions. *Ken Jubb*

*Right:* The only red pre-production LD was that allocated to West Yorkshire as DX2 (MWR 618). This head-on photograph shows in detail the entirely new bonnet design, with slotted grille featuring both Bristol and ECW badges. Winding-handles for the route indicators are visible under the canopy, although some operators specified that these be fitted inside the bus. *J. S. Cockshott*

The Eastern Coach Works body continued to provide 58 seats, a luggage area being retained over the rear wheel arches. Deeper windows in the style of the second prototype were also retained, although the front profile was more curved than on previous ECW double-deckers. Uniformity of window length for each main side bay was introduced, in contrast to the prototypes, which had extended windows above the rear wheel arches. Overall height, naturally, remained as before, while weight had increased just a little, to 7 tons 10½cwt.

The pre-production models were immediately circulated among the Tilling group of companies, Bristol's own example (PHW 958) being loaned to Red & White from May to June 1953, while Western National's (OTT 2) was borrowed by Brighton, Hove & District and Thames Valley before entering service with its intended owner. Hants & Dorset's LRU 67 was demonstrated to Wilts & Dorset and Southern Vectis, Crosville's RFM 406 operating simultaneously

*Right:* Western National's 1863 (OTT 2) operated on Brighton, Hove & District's service 38 during July 1953, before it reached the West Country. It was well laden when captured by the camera heading for Brighton's seafront, although orders from BH&D remained conspicuously absent. *B. L. Jackson collection*

with Midland General. Meanwhile, in the North of England, West Yorkshire's MWR 618 visited Cumberland and United Automobile Services.

The introduction of six LDs ahead of the main production run demonstrated a thoroughness of testing which was to ensure the final production model would be as efficient and reliable as possible. Such testing was usual practice for Bristol/ECW products, but manufacturers that failed to test models so thoroughly did not enjoy Bristol's reputation for dependability.

The operation of the pre-production Lodekkas resulted in yet more modifications and refinements, full LD production eventually getting underway from September 1953, a month later than planned, owing to last-minute design improvements and continuing difficulties with supplies of new materials. From this point, however, Lodekkas were to be introduced throughout Britain in their hundreds.

*Left:* For many years both Southern and Western National published timetables with a cover illustration of a bus bursting through a map of the West of England. The artwork was updated from time to time, until pre-production Lodekka OTT 2 was used to represent the contemporary double-decker, as seen on this Wiltshire Area publication from 1958.

*Below:* Hants & Dorset 1337 (LRU 67) stands at Bournemouth bus station in later life, surrounded by production LDs. As can be seen, this operator fitted sun visors over the cab windscreens of its vehicles, while the upper cream bands have also been dispensed with. LRU 67 remained in regular service with H&D for well over 20 years. *John May*

# 4 Production LDs

An early LD chassis, finished in silver with the bonnet assembly in position, stands at Arno's Castle, Brislington. It was in this form, with the driver exposed to the elements in all weather conditions, that all Lodekka chassis were driven the 265 miles to Lowestoft, the most easterly town in Britain. *Bristol Tramways*

WITH full production of the Lodekka underway, the first examples of Bristol's new double-decker chassis were delivered to Eastern Coach Works in Lowestoft towards the end of November 1953.

The company minutes record that arrangements were made with ECW to adjust the delivery programme, to take account of the 'unavoidable arrears' of this type that had accrued. The 100th sanction continued with the production LDs and ran until November 1954, comprising 200 chassis. These were powered by either Bristol's own engine or Gardner power units. Of the latter the vast majority were six-cylinder 6LW units, although a few companies opted for the less powerful five-cylinder Gardner 5LW. Chassis designations were LD6B, LD6G or LD5G, depending on the power unit fitted.

Appropriately the first production chassis (chassis 100.007) was destined for Crosville Motor Services, of Chester, as ML662 (RFM 407). Crosville's operating territory included Liverpool and extended throughout much of North Wales, and the company rapidly became the largest

customer for LDs. Indeed, it would ultimately take more Lodekkas of various types than any other operator, including Bristol itself.

The production LDs were similar to the six pre-production examples, although a number of refinements were introduced. The most noticeable concerned the grille and front cowl. Concealing the radiator and engine inside metal or glass fibre panelling was becoming fashionable at this time — it gave a more modern appearance, and a number of bus manufacturers were adopting this approach. Unfortunately, the bonnet line tended to be wider and therefore restricted the driver's view of the nearside kerb to a greater extent than a bus with an exposed radiator. Production Bristol Lodekkas thus had a slightly lower bonnet line than that of the pre-production models, through a greater curvature across the top of the front cowl which resulted in a lower front nearside edge. The lower edge of the driver's windscreen was also

a little more curved, to match the modified cowl design. The shape of the grille remained unchanged, but instead of coarse slots much finer slats were used. The Bristol badges also remained, but the ECW plate at the base was discontinued. Inside the lower saloon, modifications to the housings covering the rear axle gearing could be found as Bristol and ECW strove to minimise the intrusion of the rear axle.

Joining Crosville as recipients of early production LDs were Cumberland, Eastern Counties, Eastern National, Hants & Dorset, Lincolnshire, Mansfield District, Midland General, Red & White (based in Chepstow), Southern Vectis (on the Isle of Wight), United Counties, United Welsh, West Yorkshire, Westcliff-on-Sea, Western/Southern National, Wilts & Dorset and, of course, Bristol's own operating department (along with its Bath Tramways and Cheltenham District subsidiaries). This represented the vast

A rear view of the chassis, clearly illustrating the single, offset propeller shaft running to the offside of the dropped centre rear axle, as adopted for production LDs. The Bristol scroll emblem was routinely stencilled onto chassis throughout the production life of the Lodekka. *Bristol Tramways*

The earliest production Lodekkas had deep, slatted grilles and long front mudguards, as designers grappled with both the practicalities — and the modern fashion — of enclosing the engine and radiator. One of the earliest was Western National 1865 (OTT 4), an LD6B with the then standard 58-seat body. The white steering wheel reminded drivers this was an 8ft-wide bus! *P. Hulin*

The earliest production Lodekkas had deep, slatted grilles and long front mudguards, as designers grappled with both the practicalities — and the modern fashion — of enclosing the engine and radiator. One of the earliest was Western National 1865 (OTT 4), an LD6B with the then standard 58-seat body. The white steering wheel reminded drivers this was an 8ft-wide bus! *P. Hulin*

majority of Tilling-group companies and resulted in the Lodekka's rapidly becoming familiar throughout England and Wales.

Of the first LD sanction of 200 vehicles, most were finished as 58-seat buses with 25 seats in the lower saloon and 33 upstairs. However, Southern Vectis received 21 of these early Lodekkas with reduced seating for 21 passengers on the lower deck, in order to allow increased luggage space; this was considered important on the Isle of Wight, which experienced substantial holiday traffic, and came at a time when increased numbers of buses were being introduced as a result of closure of much of the island's railway network. Simultaneously, Crosville received 59 LDs, most finished in standard Tilling green with cream bands, but eight LD6Bs were rather special, being fitted out as double-deck coaches, with luxury seats for 50 or 52, only 20 of which were on the lower deck, together with tables between the seats behind the front bulkhead (arranged in railway-carriage style), large luggage compartments and a completely straight staircase (rather than turning through 90° from the platform). Painted cream with black trim, these striking vehicles were employed primarily on express services between Liverpool and North Wales.

Commercial Motor Shows continued to be held in alternate years at Earl's Court, albeit without Bristol after 1948, owing to the sales restrictions described earlier. Whilst unable to exhibit at this important event, the company nevertheless commissioned the construction of large-scale models of an eight-wheel Bristol HG lorry and a Bristol/ECW Lodekka, which featured in an elaborate display at the 1954 Show; this included photographs and diagrams, and the Lodekka model was positioned under a mock low bridge. Bristol obviously believed this would not contravene any regulations, but objections were immediately raised by other manufacturers, and the entire display was screened from view! The Lodekka model, some 2-3ft in length, was superbly accurate and was finished in green Crosville livery. For many years afterwards it resided in a glass case in the commissionaire's office at the entrance to Bristol's main Bath Road premises, but in the 1970s, a few years before closure of the works, it disappeared, and its whereabouts remain unknown.

Whilst the Lodekka appeared rapidly with Tilling operators, the nationalised Scottish companies, which were also under BTC control, were not traditional Bristol users. However, the minutes of Bristol's board meeting of 9 December 1953 reveal that among new orders received was one for 12 for 'a Scottish Group Company'. In fact, of the second Lodekka sanction (No 104), comprising 150 chassis that rolled off the production line between November 1954 and April 1955, no fewer than 20 were destined for Western SMT, of Kilmarnock, while a further 10 were for Motherwell-based Central SMT.

*Left:* View of the lower saloon of an LD-type Bristol Lodekka, showing the rear-facing bench seat behind the front bulkhead, together with the production version of the sunken gangway.
*M. S. Curtis*

*Below:* Crosville took a batch of early Lodekka coaches with well-spaced luxury seating, luggage racks, tables and straight stairs (rather than turning through 90° at the rear offside corner, in the normal manner). Powered by Bristol engines, and finished in a livery of cream with black trim, they are exemplified by ML676 (RFM 422), photographed upon completion during July 1954. *ECW*

Right: Attempts to improve brake cooling are apparent from this picture of West Yorkshire DX5 (MWY 114), another LD6B, which was new in May 1954.
P. Yeomans

At this point a revised design of radiator grille was introduced, the long, heavy-looking outline being replaced by a shorter style which gave Lodekkas a much lighter and, indeed, 'friendlier' appearance. As this change was being introduced, operators sometimes received consecutive deliveries with a mixture of the two designs, Central SMT, for example, receiving buses with both short and long grilles among its earliest Lodekka deliveries. Among Tilling companies Darlington-based United Automobile Services was another new customer for the Lodekka, in the spring of 1955 receiving the first of many for operation in the North East of England.

Seating capacity was generally increased slightly from 58 to 60 from this time, most operators now accepting vehicles with bench seats for three (instead of two) over the rear wheel-arches, although Bristol Tramways was among those to continue specifying the two-seater design, which retained a luggage shelf over each rear wheel.

A significant change occurred from 1 January 1955, when the Bristol works — while remaining under BTC control — was separated from the operational Bristol Tramways & Carriage Co Ltd. Henceforth the Motor Constructional Works was to become Bristol Commercial Vehicles Ltd, a company that in readiness for this move had been formed 12 years earlier! However, the operating and manufacturing companies remained closely connected: both perpetuated the use of the '*Bristol*' scroll emblem, and close co-operation continued

Right: Wearing its operator's distinctive blue livery, Midland General 440 (XNU 424), a 1955 LD6G with four-leaf power doors fitted to the rear platform, heads for Mansfield.
John May

much as before; staff even retained shared sports-club membership. Two years later Bristol Tramways was itself renamed, adopting the new title of Bristol Omnibus Co Ltd.

The 108th sanction, which ran throughout 1955, consisted of 250 LDs, which, with one exception, were for existing Lodekka customers and included more for use in Scotland. The largest number for one company was again for Crosville, which took 57, while the new recipient was Durham District Services, which took five LD6Bs. Durham District was an associate company of United Automobile Services, but unlike those of its much larger neighbour, which were red, Durham's buses were painted green.

Following this sanction, LD production flowed straight into the 116th, consisting of a further 200 chassis, and this run saw a number of developments. As usual, Crosville received the greatest number, with an allocation of 35 buses, of which a further eight wore cream and black. These were not coaches, however, but 60-seat buses fitted with convertible-open-top bodywork incorporating detachable roofs. In summer these buses would have their 'lids' lifted off and guard-rails added around the top deck, for operation along the North Wales coast. This involved ECW incorporating additional strengthening around the top deck, which raised the level of the upper-deck window line. The upper-deck windows were therefore shallower than standard, in order not to compromise the low overall height of these Lodekkas, when the roof section was in place. They entered service during 1956.

*Above:* The changeover from LDs with deep grilles to those with the shallower design occurred over a drawn-out period, operators often receiving a mixture of the two designs simultaneously. Central SMT B9 (GM 7009), an LD6G, was one of the earliest Lodekkas to display the new style, although new LDs with the deep grille continued to appear with Central, amongst others. It is seen during July 1955 at Helensburgh, a destination displayed not only at the front but also over the rear platform. *Ian Maclean*

*Above left:* The close relationship between Bristol and ECW was reflected by the companies' uniquely sharing a chassis/ bodybuilder's plate from the mid-1950s until the end of production. The plate would have been seen by countless passengers, being affixed above the alcove below the stairs that was habitually occupied by the conductor. *M. S. Curtis*

*Left:* An LD6B from the Bristol city fleet, LC8273 (UHY 400), heads along Rupert Street towards Knowle West, past one of the city's main BMC motor-car dealerships. *Roy Marshall*

During this period one more Tilling company was added to the list of those running LDs, when 15 arrived with the Reading-based Thames Valley Traction Co. Ten of these were completed to coach specification for use on routes to London but were nevertheless finished in standard Tilling red-and-cream bus livery. Their internal arrangement, offering more comfort and superior seating compared with a standard bus, reduced capacity by up to five passengers.

Sixty-seven LDs from the 116th sanction were destined for Scotland, existing customers Central SMT (which took an additional 17) and Western SMT (20) being joined by W. Alexander

& Sons (five), its David Lawson subsidiary (10) and Scottish Omnibuses (15). This added considerable variety to the liveries worn by Lodekkas. Central and Western vehicles carried different versions of deep red, while Alexander's colour for its main fleet was blue, Lawson's being red; later some Alexander LDs would also appear in red for operation in Perth or Kirkcaldy. Scottish Omnibuses, meanwhile, used a distinctive light green, relieved by cream and dark green, with 'SMT' as its fleetname.

Among several detail design changes applied to the Lodekka from this time was the shortening of the front mudguards. This was to improve brake cooling — and no doubt also reduced the risk of accident damage — and soon operators modified their earlier LDs similarly. Above the radiator a series of decorative aluminium strips was added to the front cowl on either side of the radiator filler cap; this gave the impression of 'whiskers' and became characteristic of the Lodekka from this point. The cowl itself had been fabricated in three sections, but this too was about to change, henceforth being produced as a one-piece moulding. Further modifications concerned the detail around the cab and the waistband above the canopy (some of these features first appearing on Eastern National 1485), all of which very subtly continued a process of improving overall appearance.

The 120th sanction consisted of 120 chassis, delivered to ECW between April and July 1956, followed immediately by the 130th sanction, comprising a further 200 chassis which took production

*Above:* The 116th sanction included the first Lodekkas bodied as convertible open-toppers, eight being produced for Crosville for use along the North Wales coast. These were also among the first LDs to receive short front wings from new. Originally numbered MG812, DLG812 (XFM 224) was photographed not in Wales but on the streets of London whilst on hire to London coach operator Tillings Transport, in whose employ it would join other open-top buses from all over the country, with private parties aboard, for the annual pilgrimage to the Epsom Derby. *A. J. Douglas*

*Right:* Chassis 116.166 formed the basis of Thames Valley 763 (MBL 844), which was fitted with 55 luxury coach seats and employed on services A and B from Reading into London. Looking immaculate, it is seen unloading at Victoria Coach Station, having just arrived from Berkshire. *R. H. G. Simpson*

*Above:* Another bus to receive the short radiator while retaining long wings was new in June 1956. With chassis number 116.135 (revealing it to be from the 116th sanction), Cumberland 369 (RAO 733) was a Gardner-powered example. Seating was provided for 60 (by now the standard figure for LDs), while Cave-Browne-Cave heating equipment was also installed. *ECW*

*Left:* The growing numbers of Lodekkas taking to the roads was marked more than once. In January 1957 a ceremony was held at ECW whereby the 1,000th LD built was handed over to Eastern National Chairman Mr T. S. Gavin *(left)* by Mr S. Kennedy, Chairman of the Tilling Group Management Board. The driver looks on through the opening windscreen, which remained a Lodekka feature until quite late on in production. The bus was an LD5G, which entered service as 1515 (297 JHK). *British Transport Commission*

A variety of rear end styles could also be found on Lodekkas. Production LDs were constructed with either an open platform or one enclosed by manually operated two-section or power-operated four-leaf folding doors. Enclosed platforms were generally specified for longer-distance or country routes, although this was not rigidly followed. There were also differing rear-window layouts on the lower deck: open-platform vehicles generally (though not always) featured a single rear window, whereas enclosed versions required an additional door as an emergency exit, necessitating two windows.

Although the Lodekka was being produced in substantial numbers, Bristol's K-type double-decker remained in production until the summer of 1957. Latterly most K types had been KSWs, although the last eight were narrower KS variants for Brighton, Hove & District, which had no need of low-height buses and took the opportunity to receive a final batch of narrow (7ft 6in) double-deckers, which it considered more suitable for some of Brighton's narrow streets.

Sanction 134, produced in 1957, consisted of 250 LD chassis and was significant in a number of ways, not least because almost every company in the BTC's Tilling and Scottish groups took further examples. Most were existing customers, but one new name to appear on the delivery list was that of the Notts & Derby Traction Co, which was closely associated with Midland General. Trials with Bristol's new BVW engine, displacing 8.9 litres (compared with the AVW's 8.25), began when two LDs from this sanction, for Red & White and Crosville, were fitted retrospectively with this power unit.

*Above:* With crew wearing Tilling uniform in attendance, this Eastern Counties LD5G, LKD200 (VVF 200), is pictured a short distance from where its body was constructed, at Lowestoft. This photograph was taken in 1971, just a year before NBC's new corporate image began to replace Tilling red (and many other shades) across the country. *M. S. Curtis*

to the summer of 1957. Power continued to be provided by Bristol or Gardner, while Eastern Counties, Eastern National and United Counties continued to specify five-cylinder engines for operation in the flatter terrain of Eastern England.

From around this time a new feature started to become familiar on Lodekkas, the revised Cave-Browne-Cave system of heating and ventilation, whilst not unique to Bristol, being widely adopted by BTC operators. The conventional radiator was replaced by two grilles positioned above the waist-band, on either side of the destination display. These were used to provide a warm air flow or ventilation to the saloons while also replacing the function of a radiator in front of the engine, although the Lodekka's grille was nevertheless retained.

*Right:* David Lawson Ltd of Kirkintilloch was a subsidiary of W. Alexander & Sons and received no fewer than 27 LDs before being absorbed by Alexander (Midland) in 1961. Among them was RD31 (JWG 86), new in 1957, wearing Lawson's lined-out deep-red livery. It has a one-piece front cowl and sloping waistband over the front canopy — design changes introduced gradually as production progresses. Note also that this bus has sliding window ventilators, each operator specifying its choice of hopper, sliding or fixed windows. *R. L. Wilson*

The 134th sanction also included six vehicles built to an increased length of 30ft, taking advantage of the recently changed regulations relating to overall length and axle-weight limits for Public Service Vehicles, introduced during 1956. The wheelbase was accordingly extended from the 16ft 8½in of the standard LD to 18ft 6in. Delivered during 1957, these vehicles were designated 'LDL' (although the chassis-production register records them as '30ft LLDs'). They seated 70 passengers, were powered by Gardner six-cylinder engines and, as with earlier experimental Lodekkas, were distributed among a number of Tilling operators, in order that their design could be more widely assessed.

Given that the Tilling Group — with a handful of exceptions — was more-or-less evenly split between 'red' and 'green' companies, it is interesting to note how few experimental Lodekkas appeared in red livery. Among the experimental batch of LDLs there was just one, this becoming Thames Valley 779 (NBL 736); those in green were allocated to Bristol (not unnaturally) as L8450 (YHT 962), Hants & Dorset as 1406 (UEL 727) and Western National as 1935/6 (VDV 752/3), while the sixth example was finished in blue and cream as Notts & Derby 464 (13 DRB). The Western National pair were fitted with Westinghouse air-brake equipment, dual-circuit air braking having been fitted experimentally to several (and possibly all six) of

the 30ft-long LDLs. Western National was closely related to Southern National, the two companies sharing a single head office and management, and it was not long before one of its LDLs, No 1936, was transferred from Taunton to Southern National at Weymouth (its side fleetnames being amended accordingly, though not that on the front!) in order to broaden operational experience. This prompted a story in the *Dorset Evening Echo*, which described it as a 'giant bus', 3ft longer than its predecessors and capable of carrying 10-15 more passengers than other double-deckers in the resort. The report also noted that there was an extra emergency exit in the front offside window, concluding: 'This makes three emergency exits, the two others [being] positioned at the rear.'

The next sanction, the 138th, took LD production from the end of 1957 right through 1958 and was to be the largest ever for LDs, comprising 300 chassis, although eight were somewhat non-standard and will be described in detail later. Once again, almost every Tilling and Scottish company received new LDs. Also built during this period were two more LDX prototypes, which further advanced the Lodekka design, but these too will be considered in a later chapter.

Whilst Bristol was still unable to exhibit at Commercial Motor Shows, the company nevertheless found ways to display its products. During April 1958 a display was mounted at Harrogate for the benefit of the State-owned

One of the six 1957 LDLs, Hants & Dorset 1406 (UEL 727), photographed in October 1957 upon completion at Lowestoft. Revised window spacing applied to these vehicles, with the result that the rear wheels remained within a single bay. *ECW*

*Right:* One LDL received blue and cream livery and was allocated to Notts & Derby Traction, which took the trouble to add the legend 'Travel by bus – Shipshape and *Bristol* Fashion' (with the word '*Bristol*' written in scroll form) on its lower nearside windows. The significance of this was probably lost on most Notts & Derby passengers, but it reflected the interest in a trial bus such as this from a relatively recent operator of Bristol vehicles which had been drawn into the Tilling group as a direct result of nationalisation of the power industry! Registered 13 DRB, the bus received fleet number 464. *Photobus*

*Right:* All six of the 30ft-long LDL models built in 1957 were Gardner-powered. Two were allocated to Western National as its 1935/6 (VDV 752/3), but in this view 1936 is destined for Chickerell in Weymouth, having been transferred to sister company Southern National. Note, however, that although the side fleetname has been amended accordingly, that above the grille continues to read 'WESTERN NATIONAL'. *B. L. Jackson*

Tilling and Scottish companies. Hosted by the local Tilling operator, West Yorkshire, it was held in conjunction with a BTC conference and, with the exception of a lone West Yorkshire Bedford OB coach, was very much a Bristol/ECW display. It included a BVW engine, a scale model of the Bristol/ECW railbus introduced that year by British Railways, six Bristol MW single-deckers with a range of bus and coach bodywork (including at least one from the local West Yorkshire fleet), three LDs (among them one newly delivered for the York-West Yorkshire operation), the Notts & Derby LDL and prototype chassis LDX.003.

Produced from the end of 1958 to the summer of 1959, the next LD sanction was the 150th, comprising 261 chassis (including 82 for Scotland); the production register suggests an intended total of 250 was increased by 11 to meet demand. Bristol (and its subsidiaries) represented the largest customer, taking 45 chassis, and was followed by W. Alexander & Sons, which took 33; Scottish Omnibuses received 31 — a number equalled by Crosville, which company's intake included a further six convertible open-toppers. By now the BVW was the standard Bristol power unit, Gardner's six-cylinder 6LW and five-cylinder 5LW remaining as alternatives.

*Above:* It's a cold winter's day, and a Lodekka is doing what it was designed to do, passing beneath a low bridge that has insufficient clearance for a conventional double-decker. West Town Lane bridge carried the North Somerset railway line south of Bristol. The bus, on route 36, is a 1959 LD6B, LC8501 (826 CHU), from the Bristol city fleet.
*M. S. Curtis*

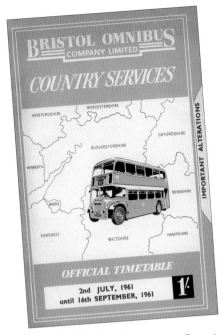

*Above:* That the Bristol Lodekka became the Tilling group's standard bus was often reflected in publicity, as on the cover of this Bristol Omnibus Country Services timetable, dated July–September 1961.

*Above right:* A rear view of a 1959 LD6G, Bristol Omnibus C8493 (824 CHU), on service 99 to Avonmouth. The company fleetname was, of course, the same as Bristol Commercial Vehicles' emblem. *M. S. Curtis*

*Right:* By far the largest fleet of LDs was operated by Crosville, which took into stock more than 350. This example, DLB977 (626 HFM), was built in 1959 but is seen later in life displaying a revised style of fleetname. The polished waist strip serves as a clue that this is a convertible-open-top vehicle and as such was originally finished in cream livery. In 1973 it was sold to Bristol Omnibus for continued open-top work, at Weston-super-Mare. *G. Lumb*

Sanction 154 accounted for LD production in the summer and autumn of 1959, and comprised 100 chassis. All for Tilling companies, these would be the group's last LDs, as preparations were being made to switch to an improved range (of which more anon). This was not the end of LD production, however, as Scottish operators were reluctant to introduce the revised chassis. Thus Sanction 163 continued LD production into 1960 with a further 85 chassis. The last of these, for Western SMT, is recorded as receiving a more powerful Gardner 6LX engine, a unit which was to appear later in other Lodekkas. Surprisingly, in 1961 yet another LD sanction was produced, this

being the 177th, consisting of 77 chassis. Again, one bus — this time for Central SMT — is recorded as being powered by a Gardner 6LX unit, while the Alexander company was in the process of being divided into three, with the result that new Lodekkas appeared with the newly-created Alexander (Fife) and Alexander (Midland) concerns.

By the end of 1961 production of Bristol's LD really had drawn to a close. In all 2,179 of the basic model had been built, along with six 30ft-long LDLs. LDs could be found in service in their hundreds throughout England, Wales and much of Scotland, but the Lodekka story was far from over.

*Left:* When AA851 (WSC 851) entered service in 1961 Scottish Omnibuses' livery remained light green with cream bands. Its upper cream band was not continued across the front owing to the Cave-Browne-Cave grilles, fitted in this case with covers. Flashing trafficators had also appeared on the lower waistband; others were, of course, fitted to the rear. *Photobus*

*Below:* Bristol LD production continued until 1961, the last being built for Scottish companies, which appeared reluctant to switch to the revised Lodekka models. Based on chassis 177.069, the final LD for Central SMT was B129 (CGM 129), here seen in Glasgow during the summer of 1975. *M. S. Curtis*

*Above:* An older LD6G delivered to Scottish Omnibuses was NSG 789, which entered service as AA12 during the summer of 1956. However, this photograph shows it after transfer to another Scottish company, Highland, in which fleet it became L10. Note that in this case, as per its original livery style, neither of the cream bands is continued around the front of the vehicle. *Ken Jubb*

*Above:* The BTC display at Harrogate in April 1958. All but one of the vehicles are Bristols, the exception being the small Bedford OB coach second from left. Among a selection of types, including MW single-deck buses and coaches, are several Lodekkas, including a York-West Yorkshire LD and Notts & Derby's LDL. In the centre are a scale-model railbus, a Bristol BVW engine and experimental Lodekka chassis LDX.003. *Paul Lacey collection*

*Left:* Bus depots up and down the country could often be found full of Bristol Lodekkas. This impressive line-up features some of Western SMT's hard-worked fleet resting between duties. The triangular destination display became a characteristic of Scottish Bus Group operators, while the colder temperatures generally endured in Scotland were reflected in the reduced number of opening windows, which were often of the hopper design. *Photobus*

*Right:* A spare-parts catalogue for LDs from Sanctions 138 and 150, produced from the end of 1957 to mid-1959.

*"Bristol"*

SPARE PARTS CATALOGUE

FOR

"LD" TYPE CHASSIS

Series 138 and 150

BRISTOL COMMERCIAL VEHICLES LIMITED,

BATH ROAD, BRISLINGTON,

BRISTOL, 4.

TELEGRAMS : VEHICLES, BRISTOL          TELEPHONE : BRISTOL 77613

# 5

# The Guildford Lodekka

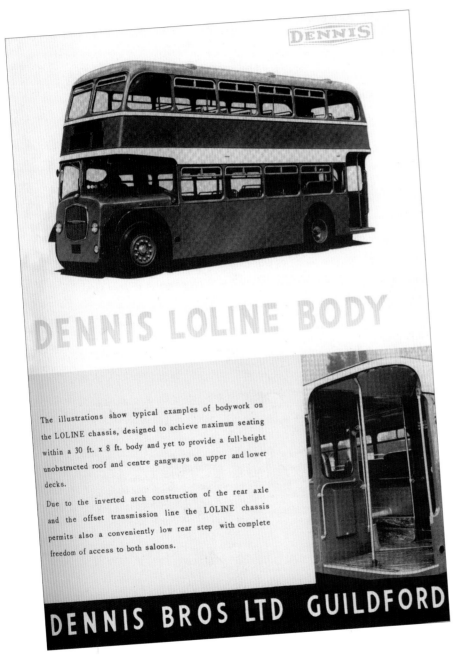

The illustrations show typical examples of bodywork on the LOLINE chassis, designed to achieve maximum seating within a 30 ft. x 8 ft. body and yet to provide a full-height unobstructed roof and centre gangways on upper and lower decks.

Due to the inverted arch construction of the rear axle and the offset transmission line the LOLINE chassis permits also a conveniently low rear step with complete freedom of access to both saloons.

**Early Dennis Loline publicity clearly used illustrations of an ECW-bodied Bristol Lodekka with an artist's impression of a Dennis grille grafted onto its front cowl! Such images appeared in brochures and the contemporary trade press.**

WITHIN a short period of time the Lodekka had proved itself a great success. In many respects this must have been immensely frustrating for Bristol's engineers, who, having designed and built a bus which so successfully overcame the drawbacks associated with traditional lowbridge designs (and which was establishing a trouble-free reputation in service), were to remain constrained by sales restrictions which placed the Lodekka beyond the reach of all bar the state-owned sector. Conversely, many municipal and private-sector operators, including those that had built up sizeable fleets of Bristol vehicles before the company's nationalisation, were deeply aggrieved that they could no longer purchase its products. With the Lodekka's reputation growing steadily, this represented a double blow, for such operators were forced to continue purchasing lowbridge buses from other manufacturers. Had passengers fully understood how the restrictions were perpetuating the use of double-deck buses with sunken side gangways and all the inconvenience that went with them, they too might have voiced their dismay. Thus, other than in the boardrooms of certain rival manufacturers, there seemed to be a widespread desire to see the innovative Lodekka design made generally available. However, with no end to sales restrictions or state ownership in prospect another way had to be found, and the ingenuity the company had displayed in solving the problems associated with reducing overall height was now applied to facilitating production of the Lodekka for general sale.

In 1956 the maximum permitted overall length of British double-deckers had been extended to 30ft, and, even before the LDL chassis were assembled, Bristol had produced components for an earlier 30ft-long chassis. This was hurriedly assembled for display at the 1956 Commercial Motor Show at Earl's Court, where it appeared not on a Bristol stand but on that of Guildford-based Dennis Bros, the long-established vehicle builder famous not only for its buses but also its fire tenders and refuse trucks. Bristol had at last achieved the display of its Lodekka at a Commercial Show — albeit under the name of a different manufacturer! The explanation for this lay in the fact that agreement had been reached earlier in the year for Dennis to produce the Lodekka under licence as the Loline, for sale on the open market. This arrangement was beneficial not only for Bristol and for those non-nationalised customers seeking to buy the Lodekka design but particularly so for Dennis, which manufacturer's previous double-decker, the Lance, had enjoyed limited sales. And although the Show chassis, built largely from Bristol parts, was subsequently dismantled while the final details of the Dennis version were refined, the Guildford-built Loline could enter production without further costly development, the Lodekka having a proven record in service with companies across the country. Not surprisingly, operators soon started to place orders.

The tie-up received extensive coverage in the trade press, but few questioned why Dennis, in particular, was the chosen partner. To find out we need to go back to 1950, when Mr A. J. Romer, who since 1936 had been in charge of the Motor Constructional Works and was closely involved in the early development of the Lodekka, tendered his resignation following the offer of an appointment elsewhere. He was succeeded from 1 December 1950 by Mr A. W. Hallpike, previously Works Manager at Dennis Bros. Four years later Hallpike was joined by Mr H. W. Chant, also from Dennis Bros, who was initially appointed Assistant to the Works Manager at Bristol, taking over as Works Manager at the end of the year, when that position became vacant due to retirement. So it was that by 1956 links between Brislington and Guildford were well established.

Among the few changes made by Dennis to the Lodekka design was the inclusion of its own five-speed, constant-mesh gearbox (four- or six-speed versions also being listed). With Gardner 6LW engine coupled to the gearbox by Dennis's established design of clutch, the axis of the engine and gearbox was inclined very slightly to the offside, in order to bring the transmission line sufficiently close to its required offside position. A not dissimilar arrangement had been adopted on production Lodekkas, with the engine-line angled almost imperceptibly by 6°.

The option of a Dennis engine as an alternative to the 6LW was offered but not taken up by operators, although later Lolines were to appear with variously Gardner 6LX, AEC AV470 and Leyland O.600 power units, as specified by customers. The double-reduction rear axle was built by Dennis, closely following Bristol's design,

Aldershot & District, with the Dennis works located within its territory, operated by far the largest fleet of Lolines. One of the earliest examples built was 353 (SOU 461), fitted with 68-seat East Lancs bodywork. *Ian Allan Library*

while full air braking was included, in contrast to Bristol's established triple-vacuum servo-braking system. The front cowl and bonnet followed the Bristol pattern save for the grille, the latter being a new Dennis design which the Loline shared with contemporary Dennis fire tenders and goods vehicles.

Production commenced at the end of 1957 with the first of no fewer than 34 to be bodied by East Lancs for Aldershot & District, a British Electric Traction subsidiary whose operating territory included Guildford. Early production also included a pair of Willowbrook-bodied buses (one of which was used initially as a demonstrator) for independent Tailby & George (Blue Bus Services), of Willington, Derbyshire. By early 1960 some 48 Lolines had been delivered, customers including the municipalities of Leigh (four, with East Lancs bodywork) and Middlesbrough (one, bodied by Northern Counties), while further independents added to the operators' list were Lancashire United Transport (six, with Northern Counties bodywork) and Hutchings & Cornelius, of South Petherton, Somerset, which took a solitary East Lancs-bodied example.

Lolines for both Walsall and Middlesbrough appeared at the 1958 Commercial Motor Show. The Walsall bus was in fact the first to a Loline II specification, with an improved floor design (which will be explained in more detail in the next chapter), and also incorporated a forward entrance, located immediately aft of the front axle. There was considerable disappointment that in revising the entrance position, an additional step had been introduced which defeated one of the important features of the Lodekka/Loline, namely the absence of a step between the entrance and lower saloon. Bristol had itself been considering

*Above:* Leigh Corporation became the first municipal operator of the Loline when it purchased two in 1958. The first of these, 60 (223 FTC), with East Lancs body, departs for Bolton under the trolley wires of Spinning Jenny Street during October of that year. *Ian Allan Library*

*Right:* Hutchings & Cornelius, of South Petherton, Somerset, bought a solitary Dennis Loline with 70-seat Willowbrook bodywork, in 1958. It remained the only example in this small fleet, although in later years several more modern Bristols were purchased. *Bristol Vintage Bus Group*

a forward-entrance design and developed an arrangement which restored a stepless entrance when combined with a forward door. Drawings were accordingly supplied to Dennis in order that it might share this development on subsequent chassis, the entire Loline II run being produced to forward-entrance layout.

By early 1961 a total of 48 Loline IIs had been completed, among the customers being the municipalities of Luton (two bodied by East Lancs) and Walsall (17 Willowbrook-bodied buses, including the 1958 Show exhibit), while Middlesbrough took eight more, this time with full-front (rather than half-cab) Northern Counties bodywork incorporating Cave-Browne-Cave heating and ventilation. The Loline II also attracted further BET customers, City of Oxford Motor Services — which operated a predominantly AEC fleet — taking five East Lancs-bodied examples with AEC AV470 engines, and the North Western Road Car Co 15, with either Gardner 6LX or Leyland O.600 power units. This latter was a significant order, for North Western was an established Bristol user which since 1948 had been prevented by the sales restrictions from ordering the buses it really wanted. All but a handful of Loline IIs were built to a length of 30ft, the exceptions being those for Luton and Oxford, which were 27ft 8in long.

The final Loline II, displayed (along with examples for Luton and Walsall) at the 1960 Commercial Motor Show at Earl's Court, was an extraordinary vehicle for Barton Transport, of Nottingham. Bodied by Northern Counties to a style completely different from that of the Middlesbrough vehicles, it featured curved windscreens on both decks — the first double-decker so fitted. What made it even more unusual, however, was that its 68-seat body was built to *lowbridge* pattern, with a sunken side gangway upstairs. As the chassis was already of low build, the addition of such a low body resulted in an overall height of only 12ft 5in, making it the lowest covered-top double-decker yet built.

Also making an appearance at Earl's Court in 1960, albeit rather tucked away in the demonstration park, was an example of the Loline III, for Belfast Corporation. This new model featured a revised front cowl, while air suspension at the rear was now standard; semi-automatic transmission was offered as an option, and buses fitted with manual gearboxes received units of a revised design. With the introduction of the Loline III Dennis's customer list continued to grow, and in addition to repeat orders from Leigh (uniquely with open rear platforms) and Luton, the municipalities of Belfast (as described above), Halifax and Reading introduced examples. Aldershot &

Having been denied the opportunity to continue buying Bristols following nationalisation, North Western welcomed the arrival of the Loline, taking 50 into stock. No 816 (RDB 816), a Loline II with forward-entrance East Lancs bodywork, is seen parked between duties at Stockport during August 1971.
As soon as sales restrictions were lifted, North Western purchased Bristol REs.
*M. S. Curtis*

*Right:* Traditionally an AEC user, City of Oxford Motor Services took five short-wheelbase Lolines with AEC engines. No 303 (303 KFC) is pictured in the centre of Oxford during October 1970. Once again, East Lancs bodywork is fitted, this time with seating for 63.
*M. S. Curtis*

*Right:* Short-wheelbase, East Lancs-bodied Lolines were also delivered to Luton Corporation, this time powered by Leyland engines. In 1970 the Luton fleet was taken over by the local NBC operator, United Counties, which already had a large fleet of Lodekkas. Pictured at Stopsley after a repaint in Tilling green is United Counties 823 (163 ANM), formerly Luton 163. *Photobus*

District ordered 107 Loline IIIs, and North Western 35. One was also exported, to China Motor Bus, of Hong Kong. The list of bodybuilders was joined by Alexander, and Weymann, each bringing its own individual style to the model, while Neepsend, by now owned by East Lancs, produced bodies on behalf of its parent company. Absent from the list was, of course, Eastern Coach Works, its sales remaining restricted in the same way as those of Bristol Commercial Vehicles.

Ultimately 184 Loline IIIs were built, bringing the number of Loline chassis produced to 280 — a comparatively modest total compared to that for the Bristol Lodekka. Two factors hindered sales, the first being that, during the course of production, output appeared to falter on occasions as the company seemed to lose interest. This inevitably conveyed a lack of confidence to some customers and was reflected by the Loline's failure to appear at the 1962 Earl's Court Show. However, it was back for one last time in 1964, when a Weymann-bodied example for Aldershot & District was displayed on the coachbuilder's stand, while a Northern Counties-bodied demonstrator was available in the demonstration park.

The second factor affecting sales was that although Dennis led the field on the open market when it revealed the Loline, other manufacturers were to some extent catching up and soon launched their own rival low-height designs, with varying success. These included the chassisless AEC/Park Royal Bridgemaster and the later AEC

*Above:* **Making its debut at the 1960 Commercial Motor Show was the extraordinary Northern Counties-bodied Loline for Barton Transport as its 861 (861 HAL). As well as featuring curved windscreens on both decks this vehicle was built to a height of just 12ft 5in, made possible by the use of a sunken side gangway in lowbridge style on the upper deck. The result was unique.** *Ian Allan Library*

*Left:* **In 1961 Leigh Corporation added a further pair of Dennis Lolines — the only Loline IIIs built with rear entrances. Leigh would be among those municipalities absorbed in 1969 by SELNEC PTE, which operator's new orange and white livery was to sweep away the traditional hues.** *Photobus*

Renown, which broadly followed the Lodekka approach, while Leyland produced the Albion Lowlander (built in Albion's Glasgow factory but badged as a Leyland in England), which again sought to offer a front-engined bus with low floor, although the bodywork, most commonly by Alexander, suffered from some oddly proportioned front upper-deck features in order to achieve this. In line with its policy of purchasing from several manufacturers simultaneously, the Scottish group bought examples of all of these rivals to run alongside Lodekkas, but none presented a serious threat to the Bristol model, which was clearly the most successful.

Meanwhile Leyland had unveiled its Atlantean prototype at the same 1956 Commercial Motor Show that saw the Loline chassis revealed to the public for the first time. Over time the Atlantean was to transform the layout of British double-deckers by placing the engine transversely across the rear of the chassis, allowing a front entrance to be positioned alongside the driver, ahead of the front axle. Initially those Atlanteans built to low overall height employed a side gangway at the rear

of the upper deck, but following the launch in 1960 of the rival Daimler Fleetline, of similar layout but with a double-reduction, dropped-centre rear axle, the low-height version of the Atlantean adopted a comparable solution. The rear-engine layout became increasingly popular, and from 1966, when one-man operation of double-deckers was legalised, buses to 'Atlantean style' were to gain widespread acceptance.

One further low-height design appeared on the scene in 1959. This was the Guy Wulfrunian, which combined a front engine *and* entrance ahead of the front axle. Not a success, it resulted in serious financial difficulties for Guy Motors and engineering problems for its main supporter, the West Riding Automobile Co, which, in order to maintain services, would later acquire as replacements numerous second-hand Lodekkas.

It can thus be seen that the Loline did not have the market place to itself, and, while it shared the Lodekka's reputation for reliability, a concerted effort from Dennis sales staff remained essential in order to compete on price and availability against a range of rival models.

*Left:* Repeat orders for the Dennis Loline were forthcoming from operators such as North Western. Alexander bodywork was favoured for its Loline IIIs, including 904 (VDB 904), which entered service in 1962. Sliding entrance doors were again specified, while seating was provided for 71 passengers. *M. S. Curtis*

*Left:* Some idea of how the Bristol Lodekka might have looked with bodywork by a builder other than ECW is provided by SOU 460, a former Aldershot & District Loline, which by the early 1970s had passed to Dodds of Troon (a member of the AA Motor Services co-operative). Bodied by East Lancs, it had somehow acquired a Bristol Lodekka cowl. *A. J. Douglas*

*Right:* Viewed in the Demonstration Park at the 1964 Commercial Motor Show is a Northern Counties-bodied Loline demonstrator. Originally intended for export, it was used instead to promote the model at home, generating interest sufficient to keep the Loline III in production until 1967. *Ian Allan Library*

*Above:* Reading Corporation's first Lolines arrived in 1962. No 30 (30 DP) was captured in Broad Street operating to Southcote when 12 years old. Its 68-seat body was by East Lancs. *M. S. Curtis*

*Right:* The final Dennis Lolines, for Reading and Halifax, were fitted with Bristol rear axles. Reading 81 displays the '*Bristol*' emblem on its rear hub while parked at its operator's Mill Lane depot during June 1974. *M. S. Curtis*

*Above:* A rear view of Reading Loline 76 (GRD 576D), one of a batch of eight delivered in 1966, showing the rear-end styling of the East Lancs bodywork and the position of the fuel tank. *M. S. Curtis*

*Left:* Two 1965 Aldershot & District Dennis Loline IIIs, 503/6 (AAA 503/6C), each with 68-seat Weymann bodywork, stand side-by-side in the company of closely related Hants & Dorset Bristol/ECW FLF 1540 (GLJ 748D). Happily, all three vehicles are preserved. *M. S. Curtis*

The Guildford Lodekka

# 6 Flat floors

IN 1958 Bristol Commercial Vehicles produced two further experimental Lodekkas, which continued the prototype-chassis-numbering sequence as LDX.003 and LDX.004. These vehicles incorporated an extensively revised chassis design, the result of which was the elimination of the sunken lower-saloon gangway, permitting a completely flat lower-deck floor. This was achieved following further close collaboration with Eastern Coach Works which involved reducing the depth of the chassis members but reinforcing the trusses forming the body sides by a corresponding amount. In addition, new wheel-arch members were created to support more of the body load, which meant that window length was no longer dependent on cross-member and frame spacing. Finally, the platform support extensions to the rear of the chassis were dispensed with, this area now being supported by the framework of the body. Increasing use was made of aluminium alloy and plastic mouldings throughout the bodywork, both to reduce weight and to ease assembly. Naturally, with the arrangement for Dennis to build Lodekkas under licence by this time firmly established, these design improvements were shared with the Guildford factory.

The semi-elliptic leaf springs previously fitted on Lodekkas were replaced at the rear by air suspension, which not only offered a superior ride quality but also maintained the rear platform at a constant level, the air supply being linked to a Westinghouse air-braking system. In addition the fuel tank was now located behind the driving position rather than mid-way along the offside.

Chassis LDX.003 (that displayed at Harrogate during April 1958) was constructed during March, the finished bus appearing before the trade press during late summer of that year, as Crosville DLG949 (285 HFM). It was a 27ft-long, 60-seater with 16ft 11in wheelbase, built to what was effectively an updated LD specification, but the revised designation LDS was now applied to indicate the shorter option. It was followed by a 30ft-long, 70-seat example which became Eastern National 1541 (236 LNO). This had a wheelbase of 19ft 2in, an increase of 8in compared with the 30ft-long Lodekkas of the previous year. Once again, the new longer chassis received the designation LDL, although it differed substantially from the earlier Lodekkas given the same type letters.

The bodies of both the short and long models incorporated main side windows which were slightly longer than those fitted to LDs. Such windows had already been seen on the six 1957 LDLs but on the 27ft-long version resulted in the elimination of the small quarter window adjacent to the rear platform. In the case of both models the position of the rear axle was no longer constrained by window-pillar spacing.

Both experimental buses were powered by Gardner engines, and both — yet again — were finished in Tilling green and cream. The Eastern National vehicle had a conventional radiator grille which perpetuated the established Lodekka 'look', but the Crosville bus offered a different frontal appearance. As this vehicle was fitted with Cave-Browne-Cave heating and ventilation (with heat exchangers positioned at the front above the waist, effectively replacing a conventional radiator ahead of the engine), a conventional grille was considered unnecessary. The front cowl was therefore devoid of the usual radiator grille, instead carrying the winged Bristol/ECW device more commonly associated with Bristol single-deck buses and coaches. This looked rather strange, especially as the 'whiskers' on either side of the water filler were also retained, and in the eyes of some observers lent the vehicle the appearance of a trolleybus, conveying as it did the impression that the bus was not fitted with a conventional engine.

Other development work ongoing during this period involved the Department of Aeronautical Engineering at Bristol University, which had been conducting wind-tunnel tests on Bristol/ECW designs on behalf of BCV. This was achieved by using 1:12-scale models of the Lodekka and MW

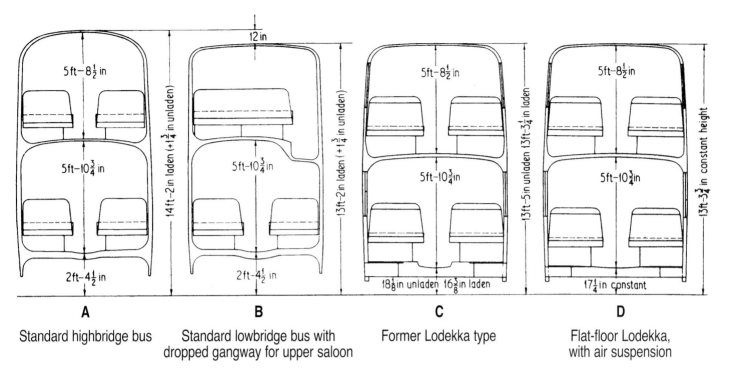

| A | B | C | D |
|---|---|---|---|
| Standard highbridge bus | Standard lowbridge bus with dropped gangway for upper saloon | Former Lodekka type | Flat-floor Lodekka, with air suspension |

*Above:* A height diagram clearly illustrating the differences between highbridge and lowbridge layouts, the latter matched by both the original LD and the later, flat-floor Lodekkas.

*Left:* A view of the rear of a flat-floor Lodekka chassis, illustrating the rear wheel-arch members and one of the air-suspension units. In later years many operators decided to replace the air suspension with coil springs. *BCV*

*Above:* Prototype LDX.003 was the first Lodekka built to the flat-floor design. It featured longer side windows than the LD model, hopper-style window vents, a manually-operated platform door and, having CBC heating and ventilating, was fitted with a plain cowl with Bristol-ECW winged motif in lieu of a conventional grille. Given the type designation LDS (which on later models became FS), it joined Crosville as DLG949 (284 HFM). This photograph was taken during September 1958 upon completion of the bodywork. *ECW*

*Right:* LDX.004 was designated LDL and became Eastern National 1541 (236 LNO). It is viewed outside Victoria station, Southend-on-Sea with driver and passengers about to disembark following a journey on route 251 from Wood Green. Seating for 70 passengers was provided within its 30ft-long body. When new this bus served as a demonstrator, operating as far north as Grangemouth in the employ of W. Alexander & Sons. *R. H. G. Simpson*

Bristol *LODEKKA*

A production batch of eight LDS types was built in 1958/9 for Brighton, Hove & District. These featured large destination displays and London-style trafficator 'ears', while plain cowls with wings were again fitted (although BH&D soon replaced these with standard front panels incorporating conventional grilles). No 1 (OPN 801) was among three of the batch completed as convertible open-toppers and finished in cream livery for the seafront service. *R. H. G. Simpson*

(the latter having by this time replaced the LS as Bristol's principal single-deck model) together with a railcar. Experiments were carried out in order to assess wind resistance and drag with varying corner radii front and rear and with a full front on the Lodekka to eliminate the recess above the engine bonnet. Tests were also conducted with the fairing-in of vehicle fronts.

Unlike the Loline (which in some cases received full-front bodywork) the Lodekka was never to lose its half cab — no doubt engine accessibility was considered more important than aerodynamics, and service buses were, after all, not vehicles that generally travelled at high speeds. Even the Preston by-pass, Britain's first motorway, was not to open until December 1958, so it would be some years before sustained high-speed running of buses and coaches became commonplace. However, considerable data was gathered which may have influenced ECW, since its vehicles became even more carefully designed over the next decade with very attractive clean lines, gentle curves and an absence of unnecessary detail.

Meanwhile Lodekka output continued apace, and at the end of the 138th sanction (as mentioned briefly in Chapter 4) eight rather special vehicles were produced. Powered by BVW engines, these were 'production' versions of the LDS design and were constructed from the end of 1958 into early 1959, the chassis being delivered to ECW during January and February 1959. The recipient of these buses was the only Tilling bus operator never to have purchased Lodekkas before — the Brighton, Hove & District Omnibus Co. This had its roots firmly in London-based Thomas Tilling Ltd, and therefore had much stronger links with London than other companies within what later became the Tilling organisation. The London influence was apparent on its first Lodekkas, which had large destination displays, unlike those of any other Tilling company, including on the nearside over the platform. London-style slot-in running numbers were fitted to the bodywork, while flashing indicators mounted towards the front of these buses were of the London Transport 'ears' type, exactly like those of London Routemasters and RTs. That three of the batch were convertible open-toppers, finished in cream livery, was particularly appropriate, for it was BH&D that, arguably, had invented the open-top seaside bus in the mid-1930s. Brighton's LDS types were not the first Lodekkas operated by the company, as both West Yorkshire's LDX prototype and Western National's pre-production example had been borrowed when new. In the meantime, however, it had continued to take delivery of Bristol K-series buses, having no requirement for low-height double-deckers; moreover the Lodekka was considered too wide for some routes, and, it has been suggested, there was a dislike of the sunken lower-saloon gangway. That it was Brighton which received this special batch of flat-floor Lodekkas was, therefore, particularly significant.

Full production of flat-floor Lodekkas was underway by December 1959, the 155th sanction comprising 100 chassis to LDS specification but now designated FS (**F**lat floor, **S**hort wheelbase). Seventeen were supplied to Brighton, Hove & District (including five more with convertible-open-top bodywork), while others went to Bristol Omnibus, Crosville, Eastern Counties, Eastern National, Hants & Dorset, Lincolnshire, Mansfield District, Midland General, Southern Vectis, United Auto, United Counties, United Welsh, West Yorkshire and Western National. All were 60-seaters, and, as the direct successor to the LD, the type settled instantly into the Tilling fleets. Before FS production commenced, however, two further prototype Lodekkas were produced which, rather than continuing the LDX series for experimental chassis, were allocated numbers at the beginning of Sanction 156.

Chassis 156.001 was despatched to ECW during July 1959. This was a 30ft-long, forward-entrance model with the type designation FLF (**F**lat floor, **L**ong wheelbase, **F**orward entrance). Unlike the first Loline built to this arrangement there was no intermediate step at the entrance, which led straight into the lower saloon, but, in common with many forward-entrance Lolines, an air-operated sliding door was fitted. Modifications to the chassis, with extra framework on the nearside to support the forward platform at a low level, enabled the stepless entrance to be achieved. Rearward-ascending stairs were positioned behind the driver's cab, the lower steps covering the clutch/gearbox area.

The body profile was altogether more upright compared with rear-entrance Lodekkas, while at the rear, in addition to the upper-deck emergency window, an emergency door was located in the centre of the rear bulkhead. To facilitate this the ECW designers distinctively placed three upright windows across the rear of the body. Upon completion this bus received green livery as Bristol Omnibus LC8540 (995 EHW) and was pictured in the *Bristol Evening Post* of 29 October 1959, when it was inspected by transport chiefs from both Bristol Omnibus and the local council. It was also demonstrated more widely to Scottish and Tilling companies. A single-step, forward entrance with sliding door was also fitted to chassis 156.002, which was driven to ECW for bodying during early September 1959. This was a shorter version of the design, known as the FSF, and was finished in the red livery of the West Yorkshire Road Car Co as DX82 (YWW 77), the forward-entrance prototypes repeating the allocation of the original LDXs. Both vehicles were equipped with Cave-Browne-Cave heating and ventilation, but conventional cowls with grilles were fitted. Indeed, within a short time Brighton, Hove & District's LDS types also had their winged cowls replaced by conventional grille arrangements to improve ventilation, as well as for æsthetic reasons, although a few Lodekkas with plain cowls were operated by Crosville. Nevertheless, even with a grille, there remained a subtle method of identifying a flat-floor Lodekka as it approached. On standard LDs two steps were located either

Although the plain cowl for CBC-fitted Lodekkas was short lived, Crosville ran several early flat-floor Lodekkas with plain front panels which were devoid of even the winged motif. These looked very drab, as exemplified by this FS6G, DFG26 (307 PFM). Once again, the flashing indicators remain in the original position on the waistband, behind engine and cab. *Ken Jubb*

*Right:* The forward-entrance Lodekka prototypes were not given chassis numbers in the LDX series. Instead, they initiated the 156th sanction, 156.001 being the first FLF. This joined the local Bristol fleet as LC8540 (995 EHW) but also toured other operators to stimulate interest, being pictured working on hire to Scottish Omnibuses, which later ordered large numbers of FLFs. Its sliding door was replaced by folding doors when only six months old, although the sliding design was subsequently favoured for many Dennis Lolines. *Jim Thomson*

*Below:* 995 EHW in later life, entering the Centre from Baldwin Street during July 1971 while operating Bristol city route 5. Not only had folding doors been fitted by this time, but its hopper windows had been replaced by sliders, the CBC grilles had received neat covers, and the bus itself was now numbered C7000. Following withdrawal in 1976 this vehicle was exported to Hawaii. *M. S. Curtis*

Flat floors

*Above:* Chassis number 156.002 was allocated to the prototype FSF, which was painted in red livery for West Yorkshire. It too had a sliding door which was later replaced by folding, four-leaf jack-knife entrance doors. As No DX82 (YWW 77) it ran for West Yorkshire until 1967, when it was exchanged for a United Auto FS of similar age, in the interests of standardisation for both fleets. Like the prototype FLF, it was powered by a Bristol engine. *ECW*

*Right:* A Bristol Commercial Vehicles booklet designed to encourage boys to apply for apprenticeships with the company. An FLF chassis is featured on the cover.

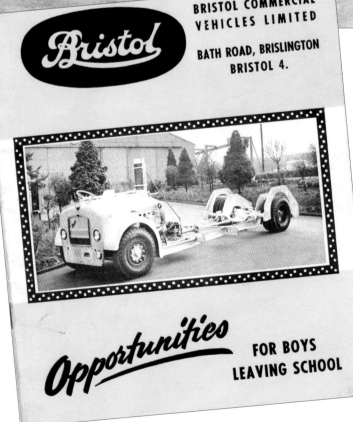

*Bristol*

**BRISTOL COMMERCIAL VEHICLES LIMITED**

**BATH ROAD, BRISLINGTON BRISTOL 4.**

*Opportunities* **FOR BOYS LEAVING SCHOOL**

side of the front numberplate to help mechanics look under the bonnet and to enable crews to reach the winding gear (in companies where this remained outside) for the destination display, but flat-floor Lodekkas (together with the six original LDLs) had just one, double-width step, to the nearside of the registration plate.

The growing popularity of forward entrances stemmed partly from the desire to transfer control of the platform to the driver, leaving conductors free to concentrate on collecting fares from the increasing number of passengers, particularly on higher-capacity buses. This was not universal, however, the conducting staff of some companies retaining full responsibility for passengers boarding and alighting — even on forward-entrance buses. On such types considerable attention was paid to passenger flow and ease of access to the platform area, which was in danger of becoming considerably slower than on rear-platform vehicles. The sliding door was also considered cumbersome and was replaced on both prototypes by faster-acting, 'jack-knife' folding doors, which became standard, although one batch of Thames Valley FLFs retained sliding doors throughout their lives.

Production versions of both lengths of forward-entrance Lodekka followed from March 1960 with the 156th sanction, totalling just 20 chassis comprising 13 FLFs and six FSFs for the Bristol group, together with one FLF for Thames Valley. Thereafter separate sanction numbers were used for each chassis variant.

In May 1960 production commenced of the 166th sanction, which comprised 90 further FS types and added Cumberland to the list of owners, together with the first Scottish operator of the type, Western SMT.

It was to be September 1960 before a 70-seat, long-wheelbase, rear-entrance version — the FL type — was built, the first such sanction being the 168th, which ran until August 1961 but totalled just 30 vehicles. Customers were Red & White (20), Lincolnshire (five) and Hants & Dorset (three), the remaining two being allocated to Western SMT in Scotland, following a visit north of the border during 1959 by similar LDX.004.

The specification for production F-series (flat-floor) Lodekkas included an air/hydraulic braking system consisting of Clayton Dewandre or Westinghouse air equipment with Lockheed hydraulic units. As with LDs, four- or five-speed gearboxes were offered, while in contrast to accounts in the trade press, overall length was listed as 27ft 4in for the shorter versions against 30ft for the extended models.

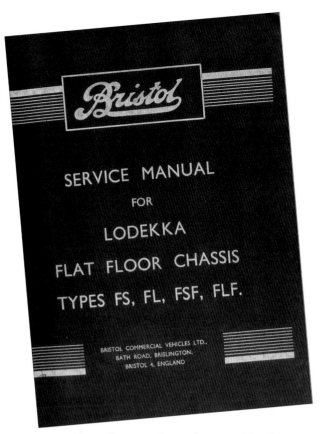

*Above:* BCV's Chatsworth Road works shortly after the introduction of the revised Lodekka bonnet and cowl, the earliest versions of which retained a Bristol scroll set at 45° at the top left corner of the new-shape grille, in addition to more discreet '*Bristol*' and '*LODEKKA*' badging. In the foreground is an MW single-deck chassis, while beyond the FLF (destined for a Scottish company) is a lightweight SU. *Allan Janes*

*Above:* The cover of a service manual for the flat floor Bristol Lodekka, as supplied to operators' engineering staff throughout the country.

*Below:* Restrictions imposed on Bristol's attendance at Commercial Motor Shows simply encouraged the company to stage its own exhibitions, achieving greater attention — and at less expense — than a stand at Earl's Court. The display of July 1962 launched the RE chassis, here on the left of this picture. Behind is a Cumberland FLF, while to the right is an FSF chassis for United Welsh. Completing the line-up are a Bristol HA tractor and ST semi-trailer making up an articulated goods unit for British Road Services. *BCV*

Modernisation of the Lodekka continued throughout its production, but the early 1960s saw several significant changes. The window rubber used to mount each pane was changed experimentally from black to cream on some vehicles in 1960, and during 1962 cream was adopted as standard. The effect of this in brightening appearance was surprisingly noticeable, and as cream was used as the relief colour for every Tilling fleet it complemented the paintwork very well. Not all Scottish fleets adopted cream, however, some operators considering that black better suited their requirements.

During the same period fluorescent lighting was introduced, vastly improving the interior environment at night, and by means of fluorescent tubes mounted behind a transparent offside advertisement panel many buses also featured illuminated exterior advertisements. At least one Bristol Omnibus FLF extended this concept further, to include illuminated interior advertisements.

The most striking change, however, was the introduction from 1962 of a completely new cowl-and-bonnet assembly, which reintroduced long front wings (with brake-cooling slots) and an attractive new design of polished grille incorporating a Bristol scroll at the top and the word '*LODEKKA*' in the centre of its lower edge. Initially an additional scroll was added — on a number of Scottish buses — in the traditional position across the front offside of the grille; however, this was difficult to see against the mesh, which was now unpainted, and was soon discontinued. Shortly afterwards similarly shaped grilles were introduced on Bristol/ECW coaches, emphasising the strong family relationship across the Bristol/ECW range.

Also adopted from 1962, albeit unique to Brighton, Hove & District, was a modification to the rear open platforms of FS vehicles, incorporating a split-level entrance with, towards the bulkhead, a lowered section before a step up to normal floor level. This was claimed to assist the elderly residents of the area but was somewhat ironic in view of earlier comments about disliking sunken gangways, as it necessitated a second step into the saloon. No other Lodekka operator specified this platform design, although many years later a similar arrangement (in reverse) was fitted to the front platforms of ECW-bodied rear-engined double-deckers.

Significantly 1962 was the year in which the Dennis Loline failed to make an appearance at the Commercial Motor Show, and of course Bristol remained subject to sales restrictions. It so happened that this year also saw the launch of one of the most successful rear-engined single-

deck models — the Bristol RE. Built initially as a 36ft-long model, the RE successfully used a Lodekka-style rear axle — not to lower floor height but in order for the drive to pass over its dropped centre, allowing the weight of the engine and gearbox to be distributed more evenly than on rival single-deck designs.

Not to be outdone by those attending the official Commercial Show, during July 1962 Bristol held its own impressive exhibition at the BCV works, for the benefit of the press and others. In so doing it probably attracted more coverage and publicity than would have been the case had it been allowed into Earl's Court! Displayed in addition to the RE was a newly completed Bristol/ECW FLF for Cumberland, along with an FSF chassis for United Welsh and an articulated Bristol HA tractor unit and ST semi-trailer for British Road Services.

The FS continued as the 'traditional' Lodekka variant and was among the most popular in the range. Sanctions 178 (54 chassis), 196 (70), 205 (a further 70) and 214 (200 chassis) took production from July 1961 to March 1964. More convertible open-toppers were built, for Bristol Omnibus (four) and Brighton, Hove & District (eight), and, whilst seating for 60 passengers remained standard for FS types, many were fitted with rear platform doors. Red & White and Wilts & Dorset joined the ranks of FS operators during this period — as did more Scottish operators, Alexander (Fife), Central SMT and Scottish Omnibuses taking a combined total of 84 from the 214th sanction.

Demonstrating that the roofs of convertible Lodekkas really were detachable is Bristol Omnibus L8579 (869 NHT), one of four 1961 FS6Gs supplied for use at Weston-super-Mare. It will be noted that the flashing indicators have been moved forward to a new standard position, where they were not only more conspicuous but avoided reflections in the driver's rear-view mirrors. This bus is now preserved as part of the Bristol Omnibus Vehicle Collection.
*P. Yeomans*

*Above:* The driver of 1962 Wilts & Dorset FS6G 638 (676 AAM) strolls towards the rear of his bus, at Marlborough, to spend layover time with his conductor on an April evening in 1969. The offside advertisement panel is of the type illuminated after dark, by means of fluorescent lighting. *M. S. Curtis*

*Right:* Following the division into three of the W. Alexander fleet in 1961 each section adopted its own distinctive colour scheme. Alexander (Fife) became a red fleet, which included ornate lining-out, as worn by this 60-seater FS6G, FRD182 (3668 FG). Triangular destination displays were preferred by most Scottish group companies. *Photobus*

*Left:* A scene that captures wonderfully the atmosphere of open-top seaside operation. With windswept conductor collecting fares 'on top', Brighton, Hove & District 2052 (AAP 52B), a 1964 FS6B, approaches Brighton's Palace Pier on seafront service 17. The vintage fire engines behind suggest the photograph was taken on the occasion of the annual HCVC London–Brighton run. *Ken Jubb*

*Below:* This FS5G entered service in 1964 with Lincolnshire Road Car as 2516 (VFE 965). Although equipped with Cave-Browne-Cave heating and ventilation, it has had the intake grilles fitted with covers of a type favoured by a number of operators. Also evident on this vehicle is further simplification of the radiator grille. *Photobus*

Flat floors

The longer, 70-seat FL model was far less popular. The 180th sanction of August 1961 comprised only three Bristol-engined chassis, for Hants & Dorset, which were fitted with power-operated rear doors. Thereafter the 198th sanction was assembled during October 1962 and consisted of 12 more FL types — six each for Eastern Counties and Hants & Dorset. No further FLs would be built.

The forward-entrance FSF did rather better, production totalling 218 chassis. The 167th sanction commenced production in the summer of 1960 and was followed by Sanctions 179 and 197. These added Brighton, Hove & District, Crosville, Cumberland, Durham District, Mansfield District, Midland General, United Automobile and United Welsh to the Tilling customer list. Significantly, Central SMT was also

an FSF supporter throughout this period, and the final FSF sanction, No 215, which took production to May 1963, comprised 11 chassis, all for Central. The FSF variant was also dropped from this point, so when Western and Southern National decided they required a batch in 1967, Bristol Omnibus willingly transferred 20 of its examples. By this time the Bristol operating company had embarked on a large-scale 'one-man' conversion programme using Bristol REs and so grasped the opportunity to dispose of a batch of relatively new crew-operated buses.

The remaining flat-floor variant, the 30ft-long FLF, was easily the most popular. Sanctions 169 (60 chassis), 181 (133), 199 (200), 208 (40), 210 (100) and 217 (200) were produced up to April 1964. Numerically the first of these chassis, No 169.001, assembled in 1960, was retained by BCV's experimental department after receiving an unfinished bodyshell. Wearing red livery, it could regularly be seen parked outside the main Bath Road works during the early 1960s but was eventually brought up to service standards and in 1967 was sold to Eastern Counties as its FLF348 (LAH 448E). Six chassis of the 217th sanction (three each for Bristol Omnibus and Cumberland), built towards the end of 1963, were fitted experimentally with Leyland O.600 engines.

Every Tilling company took FLFs during this period except Brighton, Hove & District, Eastern Counties, Hants & Dorset, Red & White, Southern Vectis, and West Yorkshire, all of which

continued to specify alternative versions of the Lodekka. Of the Scottish operators, Alexander (Fife), Alexander (Midland), Central SMT, Scottish Omnibuses and Western SMT all became FLF customers during the early 1960s. Three operators — Crosville, Eastern National and Thames Valley — specified that some of their FLFs be finished as coaches for prestigious or longer-distance services; these vehicles were finished with varying levels of higher seating

*Above:* The Cheltenham District Traction Co became a subsidiary of Bristol Tramways following the nationalisation of its parent company, Red & White. Operating a small fleet, of around 30 vehicles, it nevertheless retained its traditional livery of dark red and cream, which provided a striking contrast to Bristol's country buses in Tilling green. New in 1961, FSF6G 6037 (802 MHW) would be among those sold to Western National six years later, when that company identified a requirement for FSF types. However, it is now preserved in full Cheltenham District livery. *Bristol Vintage Bus Group*

*Left:* A small number of FSFs was produced late enough to receive the revised front grille, among them chassis 197.041, which formed the basis of Durham District DBL13 (8113 HN). Again, cream window rubbers brighten the overall appearance of the vehicle, contrasting with the LD behind, while side-by-side route-number and destination screens were also specified. *G. Lumb*

*Right:* Built in 1960, FLF6B chassis 169.001 was returned to BCV after receiving an unfinished body (painted in red livery) devoid of full seating and destination equipment. It was used for experimental and development purposes and is pictured here at BCV's Bath Road works during April 1966. Alongside are two United RELLs and an FLF chassis. *Mike Walker*

*Below:* In 1967 the unregistered test rig was brought up to service standards and sold to Eastern Counties, finally entering service as FLF348 (LAH 448E). Seen running in Norwich for its new owner, it retains one or two unusual features, including a ventilation scoop along almost the entire length of its roof. *Ken Jubb*

*Left:* During 1963 six FLF chassis from the 217th sanction were built experimentally with Leyland O.600 engines. Among them was Bristol Omnibus C7130 (823 SHW), which entered service the following year. Here, on Bristol's Centre, driver and conductor have time for a discussion on a quiet Sunday afternoon in September 1969. *M. S. Curtis*

*Left:* Fitted with an illuminated offside advertisement panel, United Counties FLF6B 639 (639 BRP) heads for Hitchin in the early 1970s, by which time the beading for the upper cream relief band had become redundant. The operator was one of a number to specify T-shaped destination displays. *John May*

*Above:* When Scottish Omnibuses took over Baxter's of Airdrie in 1962, such was the public reaction to the loss of local identity that Baxter's colours were rapidly reintroduced. Among many Lodekkas so adorned was AA 884 (YWS 884), which unusually had acquired the earlier design of cowl for flat-floor Lodekkas, matched to long front wings. It is seen in Airdrie in August 1975. *M. S. Curtis*

*Right:* The blue livery of W. Alexander & Sons was retained by Alexander (Midland) following the division of the original company. MRD184 (AMS 12B), here destined for Falkirk, was an FLF6G 70-seater. Its immaculate condition, including lined-out paintwork and spotless cream-and-blue wheels, displays a standard which many other operators struggled to achieve. *Ken Jubb*

Bristol *LODEKKA*

standards and increased luggage space. Southern and Western National and Western SMT also requested FLF service buses with lower seating capacities, in order to increase the luggage capacity provided. From 1964 spun-aluminium rear wheel discs (superseded later by glass-fibre versions) were employed extensively by Tilling operators. Such embellishments had been used for many years by London Transport, among others, and greatly enhanced vehicle appearance.

In the early 1960s the structure of the nationalised bus industry changed slightly. From 1 January 1963 control of state-owned bus operators, together with Bristol and Eastern Coach Works, was transferred from the British Transport Commission to the newly formed Transport Holding Co, although there was little — if any — change to the activities of these companies. Within this organisation, the Scottish operators were now part of the newly titled Scottish Bus Group. For Bristol and ECW, however, a further change was imminent which in the years to come would dramatically influence the management and output of both chassis- and coachbuilding factories.

*Left:* The new-style grille etc was not the only new design displayed on Thames Valley D7 (ABL 119B), an FLF6B completed at the beginning of 1964, viewed here working service B at London Victoria.
The registration plate was also very unfamiliar at the time, not only incorporating a year suffix letter (B representing 1964) using a system only then gaining momentum (no 'As' were ever allocated to Lodekkas, and many licensing authorities had yet to adopt year suffix letters) but also being of a reflective type never before seen on British roads; four of the company's FLFs, D4-7 (ABL 116-9B), carried front plates of this kind as an experiment on behalf of the Transport & Road Research Laboratory at Crowthorne. However, the usual glass ECW black-and-white plates, illuminated from behind, remained at the rear, and it was not until December 1967 that reflective plates were introduced generally in Britain. *Ken Jubb*

*Left:* An FLF6B to full coach specification, with luxury seating for 55, Crosville DFB150 (AFM 113B) was one of a batch of five finished in a smart livery of cream with black trim, with polished wheel trims and other embellishments. New in 1964, these vehicles continued the high standards set a decade earlier, when their operator had introduced LD coaches. *R. H. G. Simpson*

# Return to the open market

FS AND FLF production continued with steady output throughout 1964 and into 1965. Sanction 223 consisted of a further 150 FS chassis, in every case for established users, and ran from March 1964 until February 1965. It included 13 for Central SMT, these being the last FS types for a Scottish operator. Sanction 224, production of which commenced in April 1964 and was concluded in January 1965, comprised 200 FLF chassis, mostly for Tilling companies, but also included two for Western SMT. For the first time FLFs appeared with Hants & Dorset and Southern Vectis, while the first flat-floor Lodekkas of any type joined Notts & Derby, an operator closely associated with Midland General. This sanction also included more coach versions — one each for Crosville and Thames Valley and a pair for Eastern National. Bristol and Gardner engines continued to provide Lodekka power, although of the latter the more powerful 6LX version was increasingly being specified for FLFs by operators seeking greater performance. For the time being, however, sales restrictions remained in force, although this was about to change.

It will be recalled that nationalisation of much of Britain's transport occurred under a Labour government, but in 1951 the Conservatives regained control, remaining in power until the General Election of October 1964, when Harold Wilson led the Labour Party to victory. Included in Labour's manifesto were plans to free the nationalised sector from restrictions, which included not only bus and lorry manufacturing but also production from British Railways workshops.

Prominent among Labour politicians of the time was Anthony Wedgwood-Benn (later known more familiarly as Tony Benn), who was not only a member of the Cabinet, but also MP for Bristol Southeast. With a workforce of fewer than 1,000, Bristol Commercial Vehicles was relatively small and was certainly not on the scale of Bristol's giant aircraft factories, nor the chocolate, paper & board and tobacco industries which were major components of the local economy, but Benn was very familiar with BCV, which was located within his constituency. It was largely through his efforts that moves were made to unlock Bristol (and ECW) from sales restrictions. In January 1964 Benn

*Right:* A 1963 view inside Eastern Coach Works' Lowestoft factory, with Lodekka bodies under construction. Nearest the camera is an FS6G which will emerge as Brighton, Hove & District 59 (BPM 59B), while beyond is an FS6B for Red & White, destined to be No L9.63 (AAX 23B). Both chassis are from the 223rd sanction. *Ribble Enthusiasts' Club collection*

advocated that if every member of staff bought one BCV share this would facilitate a return to the open market. This proposal came to nothing but was followed by an announcement during the summer of 1965 of an agreement reached with Leyland Motors. This involved an exchange of shares with the THC which gave Leyland a 25% stake in the Bristol and Lowestoft companies. In the process Bristol and ECW regained their long-sought freedom to trade unhindered. This instantly created great interest from those operators outside the nationalised sector, many of which welcomed the return of Bristol and ECW products. Orders soon followed, including for bodies or chassis which were not necessarily tied to the other partner's products, for the ability to sell freely included the option to work with alternative body or chassis builders, but Bristol and ECW nevertheless remained inextricably linked.

Bristol's still new RE single-decker, in particular, immediately attracted orders from a wide range of customers, but the same could not be said of the Lodekka, despite attempts to broaden its appeal. This was no doubt due partly to the existence of the Dennis Loline but more especially to the fact that operators were increasingly attracted by the economies of one-man operation, a 36ft-long Bristol/ECW RELL, for instance, having a seating capacity of 54 — only slightly less than that of a crew-operated 27ft Lodekka. Nevertheless, work commenced on some revised Lodekka designs in an attempt to attract more customers.

Meanwhile FS production continued with two more sanctions, Nos 228 (85 chassis) and 230 (71), all destined for Tilling concerns, and bringing production of the type at BCV to October 1966. All these FS models were fitted with rear platform doors, while Lincolnshire and Eastern Counties continued to specify Gardner's five-cylinder engine as an economy measure. Excluding those designated LDS types, FS production had by now reached 890 chassis, but this was the end of the line for the shorter, rear-entrance variant; in future all Bristol Lodekkas would be FLFs.

*Above:* The cover of an Eastern National timetable for the summer of 1966, featuring the front of a flat-floor Lodekka.

*Above right:* Open-toppers aside, cream livery — or colour schemes with additional areas of cream — when applied to a Lodekka usually indicated that a vehicle was finished to coach standards. However, such liveries were sometimes also applied to standard buses which were used on special or express services, as in the case of Western National FLFs used between Newquay and St Ives. Wearing reversed livery, FLF6B 2044 (ATA 125B) squeezes out of Falmouth garage. Note that the grille mesh has been simplified, while this operator has specified side-by-side destinations, the winding mechanism being reached by standing on the step adjacent to the front numberplate. *John May*

FLF Sanction 229 was to be the largest so far, comprising 252 chassis. Brighton, Hove & District received its first FLFs from this series, while Bristol Omnibus, which had decided to standardise on the FLF for its double-deck requirements, took 47 — appropriately becoming the largest customer for flat-floor Lodekkas. In Scotland two companies received FLFs from this sanction: Scottish Omnibuses (which had by now adopted the fleetname 'Eastern Scottish') took 25, while Central SMT took no fewer than 57, with 68- rather than 70-seat bodywork, to allow for additional luggage accommodation.

The next FLF sanction (No 231) was even larger, amounting to 332 chassis, and ran from July 1965 to October 1966. It was at this point that Eastern Counties finally switched to forward-entrance Lodekkas, taking 36, while Bristol Omnibus received 60 — the highest number of Lodekkas ever for a single operator in one sanction. Eighty-three chassis were shared by two Scottish Bus Group companies, Central SMT receiving 58, and Scottish Omnibuses 25. These were an extended version offering even greater capacity, with longer rear overhang than usual, necessitating a revised rear tyre specification. Built to an overall length of almost 31ft 1in, they featured longer side-facing bench seats over the rear wheels, forward-ascending stairs and, in the case of the Central examples, seating for up to 78 passengers

(Scottish Omnibuses specifying 76 seats, to allow for yet more luggage space). All were powered by Gardner 6LX engines. Chassis 231.006 formed the basis of Central BL278 (EGM 278C), which during 1965 served briefly as a demonstrator to several non-THC operators.

Throughout the Lodekka's production run Bristol and ECW constantly improved the design detail. By the commencement of Sanction 231 the grille mesh had been progressively simplified, although the outline introduced in 1962 remained unaltered. Later during this sanction Tilling fleets received FLFs devoid of an upper cream relief band as ECW increased its use of glass-fibre panelling. Such minute attention to detail increasingly enhanced appearance, leading to some of the most elegant and carefully pro-portioned buses on Britain's roads. Many other bus bodybuilders failed to achieve such consistently high standards, the Bristol/ECW combination being arguably unrivalled, except perhaps by the careful attention also given at the time to London Transport vehicles.

Early in 1966 Bristol announced a further Lodekka model in an attempt to capture double-decker orders where low overall height was less critical. Plans were released for a 30ft-long, front-engined chassis with bonnet assembly similar to that of the established Lodekka, and whilst a dropped-centre rear axle was retained to offer a

*Left:* Central SMT BL278 (EGM 278C), a 31ft-long, 78-seat FLF6LX, illustrating the longer overhang and rearmost side windows. This bus was used briefly as a demonstrator to non-state-owned operators and is seen here outside the Bristol works.
*Allan Macfarlane*

Operated jointly with Bristol Corporation

*Bristol*

## CITY SERVICES

# TIMETABLE 1/-

DOWNS
40

7th November, 1965 and until further notice

BRISTOL OMNIBUS COMPANY LIMITED

low gangway, a conventional, full-depth chassis frame extending the entire length of the vehicle would have allowed any body-builder to add separate (rather than semi-integral) coachwork. Leaf springs were proposed, as were air brakes, with power from a Gardner or, significantly, Leyland engine. Such a vehicle would have been heavier and taller than any previous Lodekka, with a height of around 14ft, and was intended to compete directly with several other manufacturers' front-engined models. Inexplicably the model was christened LDL, this being the third time the designation had been applied to a 30ft-long Lodekka.

Whilst Bristol was clearly anxious to offer passenger chassis to suit as wide a range as possible, the timing of this model's introduction failed to take account of growing interest in one-man operation, the bus industry having little need for a new front-engined design unsuitable for such an application. No orders followed, and therefore none was ever built, but so busy was Bristol with still more new models that hardly anyone noticed when this particular LDL was quietly deleted.

Of course, non-THC operators retaining an interest in the Lodekka continued to have the option of purchasing the Dennis Loline — and some did. With Bristol free to trade openly once more this might have placed Loline production in some doubt, but Bristol actually increased its assistance to Dennis in helping to meet deliveries. A repeat order for Lolines from Reading Corporation saw its last examples despatched during 1966 with Bristol rear axles and, it was reported at the time, Bristol gearboxes. The following year Halifax received the final Lolines to be built (with semi-automatic transmission), which also displayed Bristol scroll badges on the hubs of their rear axles. With sales restrictions lifted, even the supply of components ceased to be a problem!

The 1966 Commercial Motor Show, held as usual at Earl's Court during September, represented Bristol's long-awaited opportunity to compete head-to-head with its rivals, and it is fair

*Above:* The front cover of a 1965 Bristol Joint Services timetable, which was dominated by a line drawing of a Bristol Omnibus FLF.

*Left:* Several brochures were produced by Bristol for the Lodekka in later years, this one appearing at around the time the company re-entered the open market.

*Bristol*

## 'LODEKKA'

FLAT FLOOR STEPLESS ENTRANCE
DOUBLE DECK CHASSIS

## BRISTOL COMMERCIAL VEHICLES LIMITED

BATH ROAD, BRISLINGTON,
BRISTOL 4.

*Right:* The Bristol VR, which was eventually to succeed the Lodekka, was launched at the 1966 Commercial Motor Show. Chassis No VRX.001 formed the basis of Central SMT BN331 (GGM 431D), which was displayed on ECW's stand. Bristol maintained forward-mounted radiators on its rear-engined designs to take advantage of the natural airflow, which overcame the overheating problems sometimes experienced with other manufacturers' designs. *A. J. Douglas*

*Right:* A rear view of GGM 431D in service, demonstrating its resemblance to the FLF Lodekka, notwithstanding the rear engine, mounted longitudinally on the offside. Both VRXs would eventually be sold to Bristol Omnibus. *A. J. Douglas*

to say that the return of both Bristol and ECW took the event by storm, but the Lodekka was not represented. Bristol REs appeared on the stands of Bristol, Eastern Coach Works and Alexander (Coachbuilders), as well as outside in the demonstration park. For those seeking double-deck interest, Bristol and ECW unveiled the first completed examples of the new VR, with engine mounted longitudinally at the rear offside, making this model effectively a rear-engined Lodekka that would be suitable for one-man operation. Examples in prototype form appeared on both the Bristol and ECW stands, each containing 80 passenger seats within a 33ft-long body — and this was the shorter version of the design! With Gardner 6LX engine, this version of the VR included such familiar Lodekka features as a dropped-centre rear axle, a low-set chassis with perimeter framing over the rear wheels, and low entry and floor levels. The body too was un-mistakably derived from that fitted to the Lodekka, with many similar or common parts, and an entrance alongside the driving position, ahead of the front axle. Disappointingly, however, there was a shallow entrance step leading to the completely flat lower-saloon floor and, with leaf springs, overall height had crept up to just under 13ft 8in.

Displayed on the ECW stand, the first of the VR prototypes, based on chassis VRX.001, wore the red and cream livery of Central SMT, while VRX.002, on the BCV stand, was finished in Tilling green and cream with Bristol fleetnames; when built, this bus had clearly been intended for Bristol Omnibus, as would have been natural, but something caused this to change at the eleventh hour. For the show the Bristol Omnibus legal address was altered to that of BCV, while the black-painted wheels (as applied to Bristol Omnibus vehicles) were repainted cream. Following its Earl's Court appearance this bus was allocated to Mansfield District, where it was operated on extended loan while its sister worked for Central in Scotland.

The decision not to allocate the second prototype locally may have been prompted by the Bristol Omnibus Co's preference for RE single-deckers, or perhaps the enormous capacity of these buses was unacceptable to crews or union representatives. Whatever the reason, BCV was unable to monitor the performance of one of its

The second VRX was displayed on the BCV stand at the 1966 Commercial Motor Show. However, this view shows it upon completion, still in full Bristol Omnibus livery. That it did not, as initially planned, run experimentally with BCV's local operator, became a matter of regret as the VR was developed. The VRX provided seating for no fewer than 80 passengers. *ECW*

prototypes at close quarters, and both VRXs spent lengthy periods off the road. However, this could not detract from the huge impact these vehicles made at the 1966 Show, and neither operators nor rival manufacturers could fail to realise that Bristol was back!

Despite the arrival of the VR, the Lodekka was not quite finished. The final sanction, No 236, had commenced production in August 1966 and consisted of 337 FLF chassis, the last of which would not be delivered to operators until the summer of 1968. All were for established customers, but new features continued to appear. Further 31ft-long examples with 6LX engines were supplied to Central SMT (25), Alexander (Fife) (18), and the only English customer for this version, Eastern National (53). The final five chassis for the last-mentioned formed the basis of 55-seat coaches, much of the additional length being used for luggage accommodation. This was combined with semi-automatic transmission, which became a feature of the final FLFs not only for Eastern National but also for Crosville, Hants & Dorset, Mansfield District, Midland General and Wilts & Dorset. Such vehicles employed an epicyclic unit located below the floor, under a slightly raised cover

*Right:* Bristol Omnibus amassed the largest fleet of FLFs, taking into stock more than 300. The last to be received, including this example, C7311 (KHW 303E), were possibly the most attractive Lodekkas of all, being delivered in a slightly non-standard shade of green with a single pale-cream band and Brunswick-green wheels and mudguards. A new design of flashing indicator had been introduced, rear wheel discs were fitted, and the lack of CBC vents completed the smooth outline. Close inspection of the front roof dome also reveals an aerial, as the bus was fitted with two-way radio. This view was recorded in June 1968 at Brislington, only yards from the BCV works. *M. S. Curtis*

*Left:* In addition to the vehicle plate affixed below the staircase a separate chassis plate was mounted either in the cab or under the bonnet. This example was attached to an FLF from the final Lodekka sanction, No 236. Above the Bristol scroll is a British Transport lion, a device used extensively in connection with all forms of nationalised transport during the BTC/THC era.

*Below:* Through gradual but constant attention to detail the Bristol/ECW Lodekka evolved into a truly beautiful design, as well as one that was extremely functional. The clean lines of this 31ft semi-automatic FLF6LX for Eastern National, 2886 (WNO 974F), demonstrate the type's classic appearance. Rear wheel discs, by now produced in glass fibre, provide the finishing touch. *ECW*

Return to the open market

mid-way along the offside, rather than directly behind the engine as in the case of the manual gearbox.

Whilst Bristol and Gardner engines continued to be installed, from July 1967 some of the Hants & Dorset and Wilts & Dorset allocation were powered by Leyland O.600 units, recalling earlier experiments with Leyland engines. This was among the first signs of Leyland's influence, since it had been decided more than a year earlier to phase-out production of Bristol BVW engines in order for Leyland power units to be offered instead. Hants & Dorset 1572 (LEL 656F) (chassis 236.199), taken into stock during November 1967, was the last new bus to be fitted with a Bristol engine. It did however, feature Cave-Browne-Cave heating, which other companies (among them Bristol Omnibus, which had specified this system for almost a decade) had abandoned for their final deliveries. In terms of æsthetics, it has to be said that the lack of radiators alongside the front destination display further improved overall appearance.

From 1966 Bristol Commercial Vehicles introduced a new, modern block-letter 'BRISTOL' emblem which largely (although not completely) replaced the scroll and was carried from this time on Bristol VRs and REs and, later, by its new lightweight LH single-decker. Bristol FLFs continued to display scroll badges, however, although the final few to be built featured the new emblem in blue and silver on their wheel hubs.

In all, 1,867 FLFs were built. The last numerically was chassis 236.337, which formed the basis of an Eastern National coach, 2614 (AVX 975G), delivered during August 1968. However, official recognition as the final FLF — and therefore the last Lodekka of all — went to Midland General 313 (YNU 351G), with chassis 236.326, which was not delivered to the operator until 4 September 1968. Thus drew to a close 15 years' continuous volume production of the Bristol Lodekka, bringing to a grand total of 5,217 the number built since 1949.

And then came an unexpected turn of events that was to make Lodekkas very prominent indeed, for in February 1969 they were given their own TV show! Starring Reg Varney and Stephen Lewis, London Weekend Television's new situation comedy *On the Buses* featured a fictitious Luxton & District Traction Co but was in fact filmed at

Eastern National's Wood Green depot, as well as in studio sets representing depot interiors. Several Eastern National Lodekkas were prominent, including 31ft-long FLF6LXs 2885, 2917/30 (WNO 973F, AEV 811F, AVW 399F), finished in standard Tilling green but with fleetnames changed for filming. Such was the popularity of the show that it ran for 74 episodes over seven series, finally drawing to a close in 1973. Moreover, its success led to the release in cinemas of three full-length feature films, the last of which was shot in North Wales and featured Crosville open-top LD DLG817 (XFM 229). There seemed to be no escape from Bristol Lodekkas, whether in the street or at home in the living room!

Return to the open market

# 'Another winner from the Lodekka stable'

WHILST FLF production ceased towards the end of 1968, large numbers of all the main versions of Lodekka continued to give excellent service for many more years. They would probably have remained in operation even longer, had the bus industry in Britain not found itself struggling to recruit and retain sufficient staff during this period. Unsocial hours of work and the ability to actually drive a bus (many still with crash gearboxes) influenced this situation. Some women bus drivers — previously rarely seen — were gradually being recruited or trained from among existing conductresses, but these factors and other associated cost savings were leading to greater attention being given to one-man (or one-person) operation.

Passenger numbers were generally in decline, having peaked during the 1950s, so the ability to operate buses more economically and without a conductor became increasingly important. These influences caused companies such as Bristol Omnibus to introduce large numbers of Bristol RE single-deckers rather than more double-deckers, this operator even cancelling its first order for VRs. Eastern National would go so far as to convert some of its newer FLFs to operate as one-man buses, the driver turning in his cab to collect fares and issue tickets through a modified bulkhead, but Lodekkas generally remained crew-operated.

The VR itself, meanwhile, was undergoing a rapid and radical change. Among the provisions of the Transport Act 1968 was the introduction of a 25% grant towards the cost of new buses to assist in the conversion of services to one-man, which was irresistible to most operators. However, in order to comply, bus designs had to meet a number of criteria, affecting their overall length, wheelbase, overhang arrangement and entrance design. Bristol's longitudinal-engined VR (now known as the VRL) did not comply, and the company had hurriedly designed a shorter, transverse-engined version, the VRT, which was first announced during the summer of 1967.

With no time available for testing (and in stark contrast to the Lodekka design), no VRT proto-types were built, this model instead going straight into production from the drawing board — with disastrous consequences. Many early VRTs soon required urgent modifications, most notably improvements to engine cooling. The first examples went to Scottish Omnibuses, while following batches for Central and Western SMT spent months at Bristol before delivery, where modification work was undertaken; other early operators of this type, particularly Scottish Bus Group companies, were also affected. The SBG never forgave Bristol and ceased ordering further Bristol double-deckers altogether, even though with improvement and development the VRT went on to become very successful throughout England and Wales.

**British Transport Advertising DOUBLE FRONTS & BACKS**

Prices per pair per month

| Quantity | 12 months | | 4 to 11 months | | 2 to 3 months | |
|---|---|---|---|---|---|---|
| | £ s d | £ decimal | £ s d | £ decimal | £ s d | £ decimal |
| 50 and over | 1 4 0 | 1.20 | 1 8 0 | 1.40 | 1 18 0 | 1.90 |
| 10 to 49 | 1 6 0 | 1.30 | 1 11 0 | 1.55 | 2 1 0 | 2.05 |
| 1 to 9 | 1 8 0 | 1.40 | 1 13 0 | 1.65 | 2 4 0 | 2.20 |

# Bristol's new V.R.T.

## Another winner from the Lodekka stable

Bristol continued to perpetuate the connection between the Lodekka and what effectively remained a rear-engined version, the VR, by advertising the VRT as 'Another winner from the Lodekka stable'. Despite the difficulties associated with early VRT production, this model did eventually become very widely used, and its early shortcomings appear to have had no adverse effect whatsoever on the Bristol marque's well-established reputation.

By the end of 1967 it had been revealed that the British Electric Traction (BET) group of companies, for so long a rival to Tilling, was to sell out to the THC, in the process virtually doubling

the size of the state-owned bus sector in England and Wales, which would now account for some 20,000 vehicles. Another feature of the 1968 Act was to consolidate this move, by creating, with effect from 1 January 1969, the National Bus Company as successor to the THC in England and Wales. NBC also inherited the state's holding in Bristol and ECW, but this was reduced to 50%, the other half share being held by British Leyland, whose influence in the works was slowly increasing. From the same date the Scottish companies became the responsibility of the Scottish Transport Group.

*Right:* The ECW bodywork for the VRT was clearly derived from the Lodekka, in particular the FLF. Its enclosure of the rear engine within the body profile (rather than in a separate 'bustle', as favoured by other manufacturers) was outstandingly neat but, unfortunately, failed to take sufficient account of the need for ventilation and access for maintenance and had to be hurriedly redesigned. This example for Western SMT, B2241 (NAG 592G), is seen when brand-new, in June 1969. *ECW*

*Below:* One month later, and a large line-up of VRTs for both Western and Central SMT await attention at Bristol's Bath Road works. Nearest the camera is Central BN363 (NGM 163G). The consequences of these problems would see Scottish VRTs exchanged for FLF Lodekkas during the early 1970s. *M. S. Curtis*

As before, the change of holding company for the state-owned undertakings initially had little impact on individual operators within the newly created NBC. However, before long, mergers of various companies began to occur, while a highly visible effect of the creation of NBC was the introduction (from 1972) of new livery styles with a corporate symbol, sweeping away traditional identities or colours, which in many cases had become synonymous with a location or company's operating territory. Many NBC Lodekkas were therefore repainted into inferior shades, commonly either poppy red or leaf green.

Meanwhile, Lodekkas were continuing to attract headlines elsewhere. In the West Country they were making front-page news, the *Western Daily Press* reporting on 6 January 1970 that many with heaters had been sold to other cities, leaving older, 'cold' versions in service, the article being accompanied by pictures of a KSW and a Cave-Browne-Cave-fitted LD. What had actually happened was that Bristol Omnibus had seized yet another

*Above.* Under NBC, Hants & Dorset absorbed neighbouring Wilts & Dorset but changed its livery from Tilling green to NBC red (W&D having used Tilling red). At Poole in June 1975, during the changeover, Tilling-green FLF6B 1220 (DEL 893C) stands in front of poppy-red FS6B 1139 (7680 LJ). Both have power-operated doors (in the open position). *M. S. Curtis*

*Right:* This bird's-eye view of York - West Yorkshire FS6B 3828 (JYG 103D) reveals that, whilst most of the bus has been repainted in NBC poppy red, the roof remains in the darker Tilling shade! NBC livery included pale-grey wheels, but, unlike their Scottish counterparts, NBC's engineers seemed to have great difficulty in keeping bus wheels bright and clean. *Mike Walker*

*Left:* The sale by Bristol Omnibus of a number of Bristol FLFs to West Riding attracted the attention of the local press. Seen resting between duties after transfer to Yorkshire are four of the vehicles involved (*from left to right* HAE 275D, GAE 882D, EHT 851C and EHT 116C) — most in NBC poppy red, although one retains West Riding dark green. *Mike Walker*

opportunity to sell relatively modern double-deckers, 27 FLFs in total, in order to introduce still more RE single-deckers suitable for one-man operation, thereby accelerating its conversion programme. The FLFs were acquired by the West Riding Automobile Co, which had sold out to the THC at the end of 1967 and had earlier been the prime supporter of the Guy Wulfrunian model, which proved to be extremely troublesome in service. There developed an urgent need for replacements, and Bristol Lodekkas from a variety of sources came to the rescue. However, this was nothing compared to what was to happen next.

Such was the Scottish Bus Group's dissatisfaction with its early VRTs that it sought to dispose of them in preference to what it felt were far more reliable buses — such as Bristol Lodekkas. NBC, on the other hand, was seeking to increase one-person operation, even though buses suitable for this tended to be rear-engined, which, it was generally accepted, required more mechanical attention. As a result between 1971 and 1974 no fewer than 106 late-model, Gardner-engined Bristol FLFs from NBC fleets were exchanged, one-for-one, for Scottish VRTs! There were also further transfers of Lodekkas among NBC fleets, to make the best use of crew buses in locations where they remained appropriate or to assist operators suffering from vehicle shortages, and in some cases they joined ex-BET fleets in which Lodekkas had not previously featured.

*Below:* Ironically, while Tilling green was abandoned by NBC in England and Wales, it survived in Scotland, where it had been adopted by Scottish Omnibuses as 'Lothian green'. Thus attired, with 'EASTERN SCOTTISH' fleetnames, in Airdrie during August 1975 is the former Eastern Counties FLF489 (LAH 489E), an FLF6G. Among those swapped with Scottish VRTs, it had become AA988 with its new owner. *M. S. Curtis*

*Right:* Another FLF6G exchanged for a VRT was Western SMT FLF6G B2435 (SHN 253F), seen pulling away from Anderston Cross bus station, Glasgow. New to United Automobile Services, it had operated latterly for Northern General, following an earlier, intra-NBC transfer. *M. S. Curtis*

*Below:* Of the three companies created by the division in May 1961 of W. Alexander & Sons only Alexander (Northern) failed to order Lodekkas. However, UEV 221E, an ex-Eastern National FLF6G involved in the SBG/NBC exchanges and allocated initially to Alexander (Midland), was one of six transferred in 1979 to Northern, in which operator's yellow livery it is seen as NRD5. *Ken Jubb*

*Below:* The exchange of buses between NBC and Scottish operators resulted in many Lodekkas' being replaced in their original fleets by VRTs, which were suitable for one-man operation. Among those to travel south was Eastern Scottish AA287, a long-wheelbase VRTLL model, which joined Eastern National as its 3042 and is here seen in Southend wearing NBC leaf green. *M. S. Curtis*

The restructuring of Britain's bus industry following the 1968 Act extended beyond the creation of NBC, Passenger Transport Authorities and Executives being formed in some of the largest conurbations, while several municipalities decided that this was an appropriate time to hand over their bus services to neighbouring company operators. Among the many consequences of these changes, situations arose during the early 1970s whereby Lodekkas and Lolines suddenly found themselves working side-by-side within the same fleet. For example, a portion of North Western's bus fleet passed to Crosville (the remainder being shared by SELNEC PTE and Trent), United Counties took over the Luton Corporation fleet, and Aldershot & District merged with Thames Valley to form 'Alder Valley'. In each of these cases, Bristol and Dennis versions of the 'Lodekka' design could now be found operating together, adding interest and possibly confusion, both for drivers and for engineering personnel. Despite transfers between fleets, such events ensured that the Bristol Lodekka continued to be very prominent throughout its next decade. Many hundreds also remained in service with their original owners with little or no modification, although of the flat-floor models a number later had coil springs fitted in place of their original air rear suspension, and the long front wings of many examples were also shortened in a style similar to that seen 20 years previously on the earliest LDs. One-man operation continued to spread, although the most heavily used routes were often among the last to be converted, leaving crew-operated Lodekkas on many of Britain's busiest provincial routes throughout the 1970s and, in some cases, into the early 1980s.

*Left:* Eastern National bravely attempted to use FLF Lodekkas as one-man buses, modifying several of its 31ft-long semi-automatic examples with redesigned cab side and bulkhead to allow the driver to turn towards boarding passengers. Among those converted was 2942 (AVW 401F), seen at Braintree in August 1974. *M. S. Curtis*

*Left:* The formation of NBC resulted in the immediate amalgamation of several previously separate fleets, followed by the introduction of standard liveries. Brighton, Hove & District was merged with Southdown, and briefly a mixture of colours and liveries resulted. In this view inside the company's Whitehawk garage can be seen, from left to right, Bristol FS 2047 (XPM 47) still wearing Brighton red and cream, RESL saloon 2208 (PPM 208G) in NBC green, similar RESL 2202 (PPM 202G) in red and cream, convertible FS 2021 (SPM 21) in Southdown green and cream and convertible FS 2041 (XPM 41) retaining all-over cream. *Bristol Vintage Bus Group*

*Left:* In the opinion of many, Southdown's livery of apple-green and cream was among the most attractive ever to have graced motor buses of any kind. Before the arrival of standard NBC shades BH&D Lodekkas began to appear in these colours with a joint 'SOUTHDOWN-BH&D' fleetname. Displaying its new fleet number, 1965 Bristol FS6G 2066 (DPM 66C) looks magnificent as it rounds Brighton's Old Steine. *Ken Jubb*

# 9 Overseas, afterlife and preservation

FOLLOWING their eventual retirement from normal service some Lodekkas survived by being converted to open-top for seaside or city tour work — as, indeed, did a surprising number of the original convertible models, their lives extended by being engaged on such work, a few still continuing in regular service.

Some Lodekkas found their way into the hands of private, independent operators who gladly snapped them up for further service, their low height, low floors and enviable reputation for economy and reliability still representing a sound investment for smaller concerns.

Many, of course, were immediately scrapped at the end of their working lives, but others became mobile exhibitions, restaurants and cafes, caravans, towing trucks or stores, while a few have been lovingly restored and preserved — although fewer examples have been saved than might have been expected.

A considerable number have been exported, some inevitably used to represent the 'traditional' British double-decker (usually in red livery) on sightseeing work around the world. Famously, more than 60 Lodekkas of various types were acquired by Top Deck Travel, to be converted into mobile homes and used by groups of young adventurers to travel all over the world, often for weeks or months at a time. They crossed almost every continent, a point recalled as the final chapter of this volume is being penned crossing India towards Hyderabad, where more than 100 earlier Bristol models — L-type single-deckers built in the late 1940s — once maintained local services.

The pair of LDLs which began life in 1957 with Western National as 1935/6 (VDV 752/3) have remained together for most of their lives, despite moving around the country at various times following open-top conversion in the early-1970s. Both are now back in traditional Western National territory, in the ownership of Quantock Motor Services. Finished in cream and green livery, they remain active in and around Minehead, where 1936 was photographed during 2007. *M. S. Curtis*

*Left:* This FLF was originally Bristol Omnibus 7149 (842 SHW) but is now a well-appointed café situated at Chain Bridge Honey Farm, near Berwick-upon-Tweed, Northumberland. Shortening of the long front wings of later Lodekkas was a modification carried out by a number of NBC operators.
*M. S. Curtis*

*Left:* During 1972 former Crosville DLG879 (836 AFM) was shipped to Australia, where it appeared in Victoria disguised as a London Transport bus in red livery, with LT fleetnames and bonnet number RM4 and sporting London-style wheel trims; even the grille was modified to resemble that of a Routemaster! Photographed in Melbourne in 2002 on a tourist explorer service, it remains extant, having now spent more than twice as long in Australia as it did in the UK.
*Stephen Cho*

*Above:* From the mid-1970s former Mansfield District LD 509 (SNN 77) found itself operating in Macau (then a Portuguese colony) among dozens of other Bristol double and single-deck buses. Adorned in yellow and white, it became LD205 in the fleet of Fok Lei. *Mike Davis*

*Right:* Following the end of their operational lives in Britain many Lodekkas were exported to America. A large number have been employed on sightseeing work, among them this FLF, which was new in 1966 as Eastern Counties FLF445 (GVF 445D). It is seen operating in New York during August 1999, having not only been converted to open top but also with its folding doors repositioned on the opposite side. *M. S. Curtis*

*Left:* Citybus in Hong Kong employed this 31ft-long, semi-automatic FLF as its B21 (CR 2146). It was among those previously converted for one-man operation by Eastern National, its original identity being 2928 (AVW 397F). *Mike Davis*

*Left:* Delta Tours of Wapenveld, Holland, acquired several Lodekkas, which once again received 'London Transport' livery. They were nevertheless immaculately finished, as will be apparent from this view of ex-Eastern Counties FS5G LFS68 (68 DNG) and former Thames Valley FLF6G D22 (FJB 738C). A number of modifications to the vehicles had been made to meet local conditions, including flattening the roofs to reduce height still further! The addition of scroll badges to the corner of the grilles is a nice touch. *Mike Walker*

*Right:* Another FLF in the ever-popular London livery, this time converted to partial open-top, with its folding doors relocated behind the staircase for Continental use, this example was once Eastern Counties FLF451 (JAH 551D) but when photographed during October 2002, with Dutch registration BE-17-51, was owned by Piet Verbeek, of Veen. *Mike Walker*

*Right:* Top Deck Travel operated more than 60 Bristol Lodekkas on journeys around the globe. Photographed in 2007 in Sydney, Australia, this FLF was originally Eastern National 2839 (LWC 665C). Acquired by Top Deck in 1983, six years later it received a number of replacement front-end parts from other Lodekkas, following a collision in Paris. *Stephen Cho*

*Right:* These two ex-Southern Vectis LDs (formerly Nos 516 and 521) were exported in 1976 and — with the addition of appropriate advertising — used to provide internal transport at the Heineken brewery complex at Zouterwolle, in the Netherlands. Photographed in 2002, they did not venture out onto Dutch roads so were allowed to retain their original numberplates. *Mike Walker*

Many examples of Bristol Lodekkas can therefore still be found, some restored to original condition and others much modified. What also lives on is the Lodekka legacy, for its features have influenced the design of British buses ever since. Today a new generation of low-floor vehicles is widely used, while there remain two principal manufacturers of double-deck bus chassis for use both in Britain and abroad. The first is Volvo (which, having acquired Leyland Bus, continued production of the Olympian, a model built originally by Bristol and which incorporated many Lodekka characteristics), while the second is Alexander Dennis, successor to Dennis Bros, which of course produced the Loline. Thus, some 60 years after the first prototype appeared, the spirit of the Bristol Lodekka lives on.

*Left:* A number of Bristol Lodekkas have been preserved or are currently undergoing restoration. One of the oldest examples to survive in original condition is Eastern Counties LKD229 (OVF 229), delivered in 1954 as part of the first production sanction. *M. S. Curtis*

# Appendices

## Bristol Lodekka production

| Chassis type | LDX | LD | LDL | LDS | FS | FL | FSF | FLF | Operator totals |
|---|---|---|---|---|---|---|---|---|---|
| Bristol Commercial Vehicles (test rig) | | | | | | | | 1 | 1 |
| **Tilling operators** | | | | | | | | | |
| Brighton, Hove & District | | | | 8 | 49 | | 15 | 20 | 92 |
| Bristol (including Bath and Gloucester) | 1 | 192 | 1 | | 8 | | 34 | 303 | 539 |
| Cheltenham District | | 6 | | | | | 4 | 11 | 21 |
| Crosville | 1 | 351 | | | 127 | | 30 | 84 | 593 |
| Cumberland | | 40 | | | 16 | | 5 | 31 | 92 |
| Eastern Counties | | 55 | | | 120 | 6 | | 82 | 263 |
| Eastern National | 1 | 131 | | | 2 | | | 247 | 381 |
| Westcliff-on-Sea | | 6 | | | | | | | 6 |
| Hants & Dorset | | 98 | 1 | | 68 | 12 | | 62 | 241 |
| Lincolnshire | | 72 | | | 47 | 5 | | 12 | 136 |
| Mansfield District | | 25 | | | 10 | | 10 | 42 | 87 |
| Midland General | | 46 | | | 11 | | 10 | 54 | 121 |
| Notts & Derby | | 9 | 1 | | | | | 13 | 23 |
| Red & White | | 27 | | | 25 | 20 | | | 72 |
| Southern National | | 37 | | | | | | 31 | 68 |
| Southern Vectis | | 65 | | | 9 | | | 22 | 96 |
| Thames Valley | | 43 | 1 | | | | | 92 | 136 |
| United Automobile | | 54 | | | 7 | | 28 | 175 | 264 |
| Durham District | | 8 | | | | | 5 | 2 | 15 |
| United Counties | | 109 | | | 88 | | | 51 | 248 |
| United Welsh | | 44 | | | 17 | | 28 | 11 | 100 |
| West Yorkshire (including Keighley and York) | 1 | 81 | | | 155 | | 1 | | 238 |
| Western National | | 64 | 2 | | 2 | | | 119 | 187 |
| Wilts & Dorset | | 38 | | | 28 | | | 26 | 92 |
| **Scottish operators** | | | | | | | | | |
| W. Alexander & Sons | | 125 | | | | | | | 125 |
| Lawson's | | 27 | | | | | | | 27 |
| Alexander (Fife) | | | | | 34 | | | 31 | 65 |
| Alexander (Midland) | | 8 | | | | | | 34 | 42 |
| Central SMT | | 122 | | | 35 | | 48 | 150 | 355 |
| Scottish Omnibuses | | 152 | | | 29 | | | 75 | 256 |
| Western SMT | | 144 | | | 3 | 2 | | 86 | 235 |
| **Type totals** | 4 | 2,179 | 6 | 8 | 890 | 45 | 218 | 1,867 | 5,217 |

# Dennis Loline production

| Chassis type | Loline | Loline II | Loline III | Operator totals |
|---|---|---|---|---|
| Dennis Bros *(demonstrator)* | - | - | 1 | 1 |
| **BET operators** | | | | |
| Aldershot & District | 34 | - | 107 | 141 |
| City of Oxford | - | 5 | - | 5 |
| North Western | - | 15 | 35 | 50 |
| **Municipalities** | | | | |
| Belfast Corporation | - | - | 1 | 1 |
| Halifax Joint Omnibus Committee | - | - | 5 | 5 |
| Leigh Corporation | 4 | - | 2 | 6 |
| Luton Corporation | - | 2 | 6 | 8 |
| Middlesbrough Corporation | 1 | 8 | - | 9 |
| Reading Corporation | - | - | 26 | 26 |
| Walsall Corporation | - | 17 | - | 17 |
| **Independents** | | | | |
| Barton Transport, Chilwell | - | 1 | - | 1 |
| Hutchings & Cornelius, South Petherton | 1 | - | - | 1 |
| Lancashire United Transport | 6 | - | - | 6 |
| Tailby & George ('Blue Bus Services'), Willington | 2 | - | - | 2 |
| **Export** | | | | |
| China Motor Bus, Hong Kong | - | - | 1 | 1 |
| **Type totals** | **48** | **48** | **184** | **280** * |

*Total excludes display chassis assembled from Bristol parts

# Bibliography

## Books

Stewart J. Brown: *Buses Annual 1988*
  (Ian Allan, 1987)
Allan T. Condie: *Scottish Bus Group
  Bristol Lodekkas* (Condie, 2007)
M. G. Doggett and A. A. Townsin: *ECW 1946-65*
  (Venture Publications, 1993)
*ECW 1965–87* (Venture Publications, 1994)
Keith A. Jenkinson: *Focus on Bristol Lodekka*
  (Autobus Review Publications, 1984)
David G. Savage: *The Bristol Lodekka*
  (Oxford Publishing Co, 1985)
Alan Townsin: *The Bristol Story, Part One —
  1908–1951* (Venture Publications, 1996)
*The Bristol Story, Part Two — 1951-1983*
  (Venture Publications, 2000)
Alan Witton: *ECW Buses and Coaches*
  (Capital Transport, 1989)
various Omnibus Society / PSV Circle
  publications

## Newspapers/magazines/periodicals

*Bristol Passenger* (Bristol Interest Circle,
  1978 to date)
*Buses Illustrated / Buses* (Ian Allan, 1949 to date)
*Bus & Coach* (Illiffe Transport Publications,
  1949-70)
*Passenger Transport* (Modern Transport /
  Ian Allan, 1949-68)
*Bristol Evening Post* (1949 to date)
*MCW Gazette / BCV Magazine* (staff magazine
  of the Bristol works, 1946-71)

## Other books by the same author

*Bristol — A Century on the Road*
  (Glasney Press, 1978)
*Bristol Buses in Camera* (Ian Allan, 1984)
*Bus Monographs: 5 — Bristol RE* (Ian Allan, 1987)
*Bristol VR* (Ian Allan, 1994)
*Bristol Omnibus Services — The Green Years*, jointly
  with Mike Walker (Millstream Books, 2007)

With its centrally positioned emergency door, ECW's bodywork for forward-entrance Lodekkas was as distinctive from the rear as from other angles. Here five Bristol Omnibus FLFs, with variously cream and black window rubbers and with differing standards of rear route-indicator display, stand at Lawrence Hill depot. However, this being the mid-1970s, NBC's leaf-green paintwork had cheapened their appearance, and managers were allowing rear displays to be overpainted or overpanelled in order to increase advertising space. Ironically, the most prominent messages on this selection are for car dealerships — no wonder bus travel was in decline! *M. S. Curtis*